Out on the Edge

VOICES FROM SCOTLAND

Out on the Edge

VOICES FROM SCOTLAND

Ninian Dunnett

CANONGATE

First published in Great Britain in 1998 by
Canongate Books Ltd, 14 High Street,
Edinburgh EH1 1TE

10 9 8 7 6 5 4 3 2 1

Thanks for their help to I. Grant, M. Dunnet and to
Wendy Reith of the wonderful Wendycard.

British Library Cataloguing-in-Publication Data
A catalogue record for this book is available on
request from the British Library

ISBN 0 86241 777 5

Typeset by Palimpsest Book Production Limited,
Polmont, Stirlingshire
Printed and bound in Finland by WSOY

Contents

Foreword

Ninian Dunnett has had the interesting idea of writing a book about Scotland in the nineties using authorial narrative but crucially particularising it with the voices of the people. As he says himself we often hear the voices of professional commentators, politicians and leader writers, but hardly ever are we able to listen to the people who actually work in Scotland.

In this he is true to his own beliefs for one of the things he believes in is Scotland's sense of community which desperately tried to maintain itself in the Thatcher years. Some of these communities, including the mining ones, have almost gone but community remains in other ways. The voices of factory workers suggest it. The voices of hospital workers, members of drama clubs, amateur players of sports, confirm it. Surely in such a small country as ours community will remain.

And with it local responsibility. This is partly why Scotland wants and needs its own Parliament. Dunnett quotes from Walter Scott: 'When we had . . . parliament-men o' our ain, we could aye peeble them wi' stones when they werena gude bairns' (Mrs Houden in *The Heart of Midlothian*), and follows it with a modern voice: 'Edinburgh is within walking distance, and if they ignore us, screw us or try to pass us off, thousands of us will make that walk' (James McConnell, Drumchapel). Let us hope that the Scots will talk to their own and make their own responsible.

But for the moment we have the voices of farmers, sometimes nostalgic for the old days before the absurd 'theatre' of being paid for not planting began; the railway men; the fishermen fighting an often losing battle against bigger interests; those who work for the multinationals; the foresters; the postbus drivers. These are innumerable people talking of what it is like to work in Scotland today.

And what is it like? Much of our land is alienated from its people: the Assynt Trust is mentioned with pride. But Charlie Douglas says: 'At one time we had six men on the place and two Jerry prisoners o war . . . an today we've Peter an one farmhand.' If there are abstract figures in the narrative, little details from the workers enliven it.

Much has now become containerised, computerised. There is automated machinery in the fish processing business, replacing the herring girls. Then again, 'When they started puttin things in boxes, that was the demise of the traffic on the river', according to Donald Campbell. In a Hoy telecottage, Lydia Hardcastle is publishing two booklets for workers in North Africa.

And still the voices speak, about education, about health, about the rites and celebrations of Scotland, and always there is the insistent hum of change. Much of the old is disintegrating, and the new is being born. People are coming in from the fields to fill in masses of paperwork. There are big supermarkets. There are the many strangers in our midst, from England, from abroad. This is Scotland as it enters the millennium. It will do well if through all the changes it retains its core values, above all its sense of community.

One finishes the book with the thought: What if we now had before us the thoughts of the Pyramid workers as they hauled their stones and set them upright? How little in fact throughout history have we heard the voices of the people, of the workers. Marx has written *Das Kapital* but what of the nameless ones who worked in the dark satanic mills?

The workers here have been named, they come from all over Scotland, they are both men and women, they are of all ages. They are landladies in bed-and-breakfast houses, they are on assembly lines, they are drivers of lorries and of buses. Let us end on a humorous note as the driver of a library van speaks:

'I go to old folks' homes, and schools – there's one school I visit outside Ardgay, and the children there are absolutely delightful. They are a charm, really they are. Except I've got one little blighter who's always looking for books on sex, a ten-year-old.' (George Ray, Sandwick).

It is these sorts of little details that made Pepys' diary live. Perhaps many years hence people will be looking back at this book and saying, This is what Scotland and its people were like on the eve of devolution.

Iain Crichton Smith
Taynuilt, July 1998

Introduction

The conversations which form the bulk of this book developed from a simple ambition: to capture something of the realities of Scottish life today, in the words of people whose voices are rarely heard in the wider world. In the fifteen years since I wrote my first shaky words as a junior reporter for the *Newcastle Journal*, the press has veered into a market where opinion is ever-increasingly the commodity peddled. And while this is all very fine for those of us who take pleasure in broadcasting our opinions, I'm not sure it encourages us to be the good listeners we ought to be.

This book is called *Out on the Edge* because that is the Scottish situation: on the edge of Britain, of Europe, far from the centres of commerce, administration and power, and chronically vulnerable to marginalisation. But it's *Out on the Edge*, too, because the voices in this book by and large belong to men, women and children who have never been seen on the broadcast news, or featured in public campaigns, or talk shows, or the letters page of a newspaper, or even phone-in polls.

Thanks are due to Harry Reid, the editor of the *Herald*, who first published much of the material which follows in a series which was tangential to current newspaper fashions. The conversations took place between 1993 and 1998 in settings as varied as the people I talked to: homes and shops, the classroom, the maternity ward, Broomloan underground depot, Rosyth naval base; I talked to the crew of the *Five Sisters* on the radio telephone as they sailed up the Minch in good weather. My question was simple: 'What's life like?'

And what came back were stories. Sometimes they are stories about the past; for many of the older speakers a bustling, colourful, vivid previous life hangs over Scotland, indissolubly overshadowing a less satisfactory present. Even the young only need a little imagination to picture the railway yards teeming with life again, the bays packed with fishing boats, the miners plummeting down into the earth, the glens and pastures busy with farm work, the streets swarming at the squeal of a factory whistle. With change destroying and building so relentlessly within a generation, our world is full of ghosts.

There are stories, too, of dreams and hopes, present-day adventures and frustrations, and many of the mundane details which preoccupy folk in every country – earning the wages and paying the rent, making or losing friends, bad weather, good fortune, sickness, hope, everyday successes and failures. There are words about ties to the land and the sea, of pride in community and ancestry and even nationhood; of God and the bottle, of ways of looking at money and school and other people.

What they add up to is far from comprehensive, and barely even systematic; a sketch, maybe, which hints at the picture beyond. But they're powerful things, stories, from the stock which sired James Bond, Robinson Crusoe, Jekyll and Hyde, Sherlock Holmes and Peter Pan. It was a Scot three hundred years ago who wrote of the consoling belief that 'if a man were permitted to make all the ballads, he need not care who should make the laws of a nation.'

Some would say we have reached the time to forget the stories, and get on with the long-overdue business of attending to the question of who does make the laws. For nothing looks as likely to change Scotland as the initiative to re-establish a Scottish parliament for the first time since Fletcher of Saltoun was writing, nearly three hundred years ago.

> When we had a king, and a chancellor, and parliament-men o' our ain, we could aye peeble them wi' stones when they werena gude bairns – But naebody's nails can reach the length o' Lunnon.
>
> Mrs Houden in *The Heart of Midlothian*,
> WALTER SCOTT, 1818

> Damn right we want a Scottish parliament. Edinburgh is within walking distance, and if they ignore us, screw us or try to pass us off, thousands of us will make that walk.
>
> JIMMY McCONNELL, 48, Drumchapel,
> quoted in the *Scotsman*, 28 August, 1997

For me, the experience of talking to the people whose voices are recorded in these pages has removed any doubts I might have had. Thanks are due to each one who gave time and a bit of themselves to a stranger. And it's my belief that now, more than ever, is the time for all of us to try to become good listeners. How else can we understand who we are, as we take hold of the power to write our own story?

Scotland has certainly succumbed to the consolations of nostalgia and romantic escapism in the past, and we will need plenty of pragmatism in the times ahead. But – and keep it to yourself – something else is needed too; something of the values of community and custom which the voices in this book talk about not just with sentiment, but with pride. The feeling, within the family, the street, the village, the town, the nation, that it's the people around us, just as much as commerce, which give us all the best chance of decent lives. In Scotland, we're half way there. As Scotland, we just might find our way.

Ninian Dunnett
Edinburgh, July 1998

Note

I'm conscious that there are clever folk who will damn the way the storytellers' dialect is transcribed as a literary affectation. My own feeling is that it's a better way than translating how people speak into somebody else's Queen's English. It's a sensitive area, not least because language is one of the ways our 'betters' – particularly, but not only, south of here – like to define their superiority. But the 'cultural cringe' is not an issue which is unique to Scotland. More than seventy-five years ago, Alfred Williams wrote this in a book called *Folk Songs of the Upper Thames*: 'The villagers speak dialect but do not care to read it. They are shocked and offended when they see their own language written. The townsfolk do not speak dialect, but like to read it. There is the difference.' If this book could do the least bit to close the gap between diffident villagers and condescending townsfolk, its writer will feel he has done his job.

The Glaswegian journalist Albert Mackie once told how he was quickly corrected while telling a class of kids there was no rhyme for 'oranges':

A boabby catched us stealin oranges:
Sez he tae us, 'Noo mind Ah've warned yiz!'

It's enough to make a person despair of the idea of getting the way Scottish people speak onto the page. I've taken a middle line with dialects and accents in a way which I hope will evoke ways of talking without attempting an exhaustive phonetic representation. (For example, though something like 'Ah' represents the sound most Scots make when saying 'I', I'm optimistic that the context will make the point self-evident even if the written word is the one we're used to reading.)

Earth, Air and Water

Our landscape has become a sort of trademark, a definitive image of Scotland, although the fact of it is that farmers, quarriers, foresters, hydro-electric engineers and countless others have been shaping the place to suit themselves since the first settlers stepped onto these shores.

What has also been shaped, among the men and women who've had to take on the sea, the land and the elements, is a sense of community and tradition which has stayed strong through a deal of adversity.

But while we've grown more sophisticated in our ability to exploit our natural resources, the centralising and polarising of society has drained the real power away from the people on the ground. And it's painfully clear that landowners' castles, far-flung multinational conference rooms and British and European policy meetings are not places where communities and traditions are seen as the hard-won prizes of a tough history.

Still, fashionable new ideas continue to redraw our lives from afar. The latest has an environmental agenda which carries devastatingly divisive notions about how the world should be shaped. If there's cause for hope, it lies in the lesson that the reclaiming of local power – and the negotiation of partnerships between the persistently diverse ambitions on our doorstep – can lay the foundations for a new story of common interest.

Making a Go of It
THE SOIL

Scotland is 78,783 square kilometres of unusually varied landscape, thrown up by a history of volcanoes, earthquakes and movements in the earth's crust. The close concentration of contrasting mountains and moors, lochs and glens and islands, is due to the fact that this little pocket was once south of the equator, squashed in by a neighbourhood which is now scattered to far-flung continents – Greenland, Canada, Europe.

Forget Creation, or Darwin – if the tectonic plates had shifted differently, we might have ended up chewing buffalo steaks on the shores of Lake Michigan, or praying for a drop of rain in the Spanish desert. As it is, by the time of the dinosaur which left its footprint on Skye, the land mass was breaking up, and Scotland was on its way out to the far edge of Europe, where it sat frozen under a blanket of ice while the warm, bright morning of civilisation dawned in the East.

The place must have seemed very far from the promised land to the pioneers who found themselves edging into remote and unfriendly country populated by wolves and wildcats, eagles and deer and wild boar, 8000 years ago. But these civilised folk had been practising their agricultural crafts in sunnier spots, and they came equipped to turn a wilderness into a place fit for livestock and crops.

The great Caledonian Forest which then traversed Scotland in a drift of pine and birch has all but vanished now, burnt away piece by piece as our forbears did their best to scratch subsistence from the discouraging ground. Peel away the peat and you can still find the remains of the ancient tree trunks beneath.

There's some nostalgia today for that bygone landscape, too. But the people who live on the land have always known that you can't eat the scenery.

> People making a go of it, that's the history of this place; adapting to change constantly, and never giving up completely.
> STEPHEN CARTER, 33, *archaeologist, working in Achany Glen, Sutherland*

3

The landscape here today is quite modern, but it has gone through many many changes in time, and mostly man has been the chief agent of that change. Even as early as two-and-a-half thousand BC we see evidence of considerable clearance of woodland, and ploughing. It doesn't sound very dramatic, but it's a quite fundamental change to the landscape.

ROD McCULLAGH, 39, *archaeologist, Achany Glen*

And against the odds, the farmers are still there. Two thirds of mainland Scotland is more than 500 feet above sea-level, and the scouring of the Ice-Age glaciers has left a paltry agricultural inheritance. The poor soil, bad weather conditions and hilly country of almost nine-tenths of our farmland – a higher proportion than anywhere else in Europe – has qualified for special aid from the EC bureaucrats in the civilised East.

Not that I'd advise anyone to try telling a Scottish farmer his land is rubbish. This is the terrain which produced famous developments in the science of agriculture, and breeds of stock like the Aberdeen Angus and Beef Shorthorn cattle which fathered the herds of the Americas.

It's possible, though, that the achievements have been less due to the resources than to a certain thrawn-ness in the people.

Do you know the difference between 'stubborn' and 'thrawn'? Stubborn is where you approach a constipated youngster with a spoonful of castor oil, and you say: 'Ye'll take this,' and he says: 'No, I'll not take it.' Thrawn is where he says: 'Alright I'll take it. But I'll no shite!'

DR HUGH MACLEOD, 56, *general practitioner, Fearn,*
Easter Ross

At Ruletownhead, six miles south of Jedburgh, the problems and the rewards are typical of Scottish hill or upland farms. Here, the land feeds a hardy mixture of breeding stock whose calves and lambs are annually sold to be 'finished' or 'brought on' in rarer, richer pastures. And those who work the tricky ground today know the landscape and its population with the intimacy of family history.

It's 'less-favoured area' here; better than pure hill, where ye can just have grazin sheep and no ploughin, but not like down at Kelso or Coldstream where it's all nice flat fields. Some of our fields are pretty steep; we start at 600 feet and run up to 1000. But we have grain – mostly barley, and a bit of oats; and seventy-five or eighty suckler cows for beef – we go to the big calf sales at St Boswells. And we've had sheep in our blood for a long time. My grandfather was a hill-farmer up at Kale Water, and he rented a farm from the Duke of Roxburgh that had been in the family for 200 years. We've got half-bred and some grey-faced now, about 900 ewes, and 250 hoggs – new lambs.

CHARLIE DOUGLAS, 74, *farmer, Ruletownhead, near Jedburgh*

Through all the changes which have transformed the business in modern times, it's still true that farmers are largely born to the work. And if there's something that makes a legacy like that bearable, whatever the droughts and the floods, the pests and diseases and political nonsense, it's to do with tradition and familiarity, the annual cycle, a sense of place and purpose and practical work. The wild country days of childhood implant a habit which carries farming folk through the sterner tasks to come.

I was born an bred at my father's farm, Gatehousecote, which I can see from my window here. And as a farm boy I was cuttin an balin the hay, an luggin down turnips wi the box-cart and horse – a lot o hard graft. But I came home from school, an couldn't get out into the hay field quick enough. We all hunted an point-to-pointed, an in the winter I shot an ferreted rabbits. An now Elsa's always sayin 'Ye're supposed to be retired,' but I'm no really retired. I had a huntin accident in '86 an smashed my hip, but with modern ways, they gave me a new hip. I can get about, an I'm always goin down to do somethin, help Peter in the fields or run him here or there, or doin the books. I've been one o the lucky ones, I've had a tremendously good life.

CHARLIE DOUGLAS

My father was a tractor-man, and we lived on the farm. I spent a lot o time with him, I would sit in the tractor with him for hours and hours, an I used to go out rabbitin with him, an I thoroughly enjoyed it. And even when I was workin in Dundee I was stayin in a farm cottage, so I never really left it. An now I've a baby, if I was stayin in a flat in the town I could see I would end up goin round the twist. There's somethin always goin on here, Peter's always dottin in and out an sayin' 'Will ye do this?' 'Will ye do that?' The usual thing nowadays is 'Will ye come an stand at the end of the road an push the sheep into the folds?' But I remember my childhood, an I'm quite happy to see Emily growin up here. It's a lovely place.

LINDA DOUGLAS, *Charlie's daughter-in-law, 28, Ruletownhead, near Jedburgh*

I've occasionally topped the sale or won the point-to-point, but I would say I've been the average sort of farmer. My father had three owned farms an two rented when he died, so ma two brothers an I got a farm each, an we are very comfortable. I would hate to have to have three sons today an divide my heritage. But I got the farm, an I've left it a bit better than it was when I started, which is what ye're supposed to do. I married Elsa in 1950. Her father was a farmer down in Cumberland, an we got on like biscuits an cheese. Now my son runs the farm here, an my daughter Diana married a farmer over in Northumberland, in Suffolk country. An my other daughter married a farmer just four miles away. What more could ye ask for?

CHARLIE DOUGLAS

But the truth of it is that the number of people making their lives on the land is dwindling all the time. Charlie Douglas's farming career has spanned the enormous changes of the twentieth century, when the demands of a nation twice at war played havoc with agricultural production and prices. And at the same time a technical revolution was underway which has transformed the business of the modern farm, vastly increasing the production from the same amount of land, and reducing the man-hours.

More than seventy percent of Scotland is in agricultural use, with twice as many sheep as there are people in the whole of the country. Yet less than two percent of our workforce work the land. In the 1920s, 120,000 men were employed by farmers and their families. The figure for full-time employees today is less than 17,000. Shepherds alone barely number a thousand, their jobs taken by all-terrain bikes and sheep vaccines and profit margins.

Even ten years ago, there would've been four people here. But the price of labour has gone up, an there's no the hard manual work there was. An it can be a lonely job, I mean I feel a bit o that here. In my father's day he would tell the shepherd what to do, more like a foreman. But now ye get up at seven, an go round your sheep before breakfast, an make sure they haven't couped . . .
PETER DOUGLAS, *Charlie's son, 34, farmer, Ruletownhead*

When I went away to the war in '39 we were still usin a great lot of implements which my grandfather took over when he got the farm in 1872. He had three pair o horses and an odd horse, an fifty years later they were still what we used. I came back, an we'd got one tractor by then, an a few implements. But they didn't last fifty years, an by 1960 a big lot o them had been replaced. At one time we had six men on the place an two Jerry prisoners o war, an they whittled down an whittled down, an today we've Peter an one farmhand. We couldn't pay for them. In '39 a lamb made twenty-one shillings, an that was the wage o a farm ploughman. It went to four pounds, so the wage went to four pounds, an in 1957, eight pounds an eight pounds. Then the drift started. The lambs came back to six pounds, an the wage went up to ten pounds. There's been a revolution in the country; some o the farm workers are better dressed than the farmers, an good luck to them, they deserve it.
CHARLIE DOUGLAS

I've got 900 ewes on the farm here, an I've got a Landrover, but it takes a bit o coverin. Ye cannae do it right, it's just too much. But ye do your best. Back when I had four or five hundred ewes, ye could do your job, an I was proud of it. But there's not many of us shepherds left, now. We're gettin scarce!
JIMMY VEITCH, *63, shepherd, Drumcairn Farm, Edzell*

For all the hard work, the scientific advances and the rationalisation, the strange reality these days is that the farming business makes less economic sense than ever before. We're part of a vast continental syndicate, and Europe has learnt to exploit its land so prodigiously that there are butter-mountains and wine lakes, and apparently neither the will or the resources to transport the glut to the starving. So some Scots farmers are paid not to farm their land.

Even those who are hard at work have become like actors in a theatre of agriculture, paid to go through the motions of an industry which has had the meaning removed from it by the global food business. In 1993 a specialised Scottish sheep farm in a Less Favoured Area with an income of £11,345 was getting an additional grant of £23,000 from the Common Agricultural Policy; and yet this hugely subsidised business accounts for less than two percent of our Gross Domestic Product.

> The next few years we have got these subsidies comin in, an they're definitely needed, to keep people in these areas. It's more of a social subsidy. We've just been fillin in this form, which is like a sort o modern-day Domesday. There's a lot o red tape. But it's somethin ye have to live with. I'm sure the miners would've loved the chance to fill in a few forms to keep the pits goin.
>
> PETER DOUGLAS

For complex political reasons, the decision-makers across the water have chosen to protect what remains of the Scottish farmer's inheritance. But with a new Common Agricultural Policy approaching, and farming plagued by a series of public health scares, the wind has turned cold.

> PAY-OUT PLAN TO RETIRE FARMERS
> Farmers are to be paid up to £25,000 to give up their land, under a government plan to save millions of pounds in state subsidies.
> In a scheme that has echoes of decommissioning in the fishing industry, farmers will be offered early retirement cash inducements to cut down the amount of subsidy-dependent small businesses.
> *Scotland on Sunday, 25 January, 1998*

And whether, in the depopulated countryside, the sons of farmers will continue to hear the call of a time-honoured way of life to take on through the generations – that's far from certain.

There's not many of the old families left. Farming's been through a lot of hardships, there's been a lot of changes, and people are not brought up to the traditions the way they were.

DOUGLAS TWEEDIE, 51, *farmer, Middlethird Farm, near Gordon*

Nowadays, a farmer's son thinks twice. In my generation, the majority of them did follow on in farming. An farmers are proud people, they don't like to admit defeat. To sell up means ye've failed, rather than ye're goin to enjoy your retirement with a bit o money. I'd like to think Ruletownhead will go on to the next generation. But I don't think it'd be the be-all an end-all.

PETER DOUGLAS

I Thought it was the End
of Everything
THE WEATHER

Of course, few have a better eye than the farmers for Scotland's weather. Few have to. Our tricky climate is governed by our position as the first landfall in the north-east Atlantic, with the winds coming from the west condensing into famous rain as they reach the coast.

> People from California look forward to seein the rain, because they have the idea it rains in Scotland all the time. It's always: 'Do ye think it'll rain today?'
> MOLLIE DRIVER, 56, *proprietor, Kinnaird Bed-and-Breakfast, Oban*

In fact, it rains on less than half the days of most years in the east of the country, and at worst, around 250 days in parts of the west. But this is quite enough to provide us with an abundance of that most precious of raw materials – water. Our most famous industry has grown from the water flowing in our peaty burns and rivers, and there's plenty of businesses apart from whisky which depend on a good supply of fresh water.

Before James Watt came up with his steam engine and kicked off the industrial revolution, all sorts of manufacturing, grinding, smithing and other businesses were powered by watermills whose remains linger with the weirs still punctuating our rivers. And in the twentieth century, we make power out of rain in a different way.

Much of Scotland was dark when the North of Scotland Hydro Electric Board was formed in 1943. A traveller venturing north beyond the Clyde and Tay estuaries would have found electricity on one farm in six, and on one croft in a hundred. It took a maverick Scottish Secretary, Tom Johnston, to push through the vast network of construction which put to work the wettest, hilliest twenty-five percent of Britain's terrain for the advantage of the two percent of Britain's population who live there. And the work of turning turbines with rainwater involves a particular exposure to the whims of the weather.

There's a lot of our places above 1000 feet. Up the Rest an be Thankful, the hills at the back o that; up the valley in Cairndow, or towards Oban, a place called Nant, about fifteen miles off the road at Taynuilt; up the top end o Glen Lyon; and if ye stand at Fallin, there's a lot o places ye can see. An because they're remote, some o these places take quite a lot o gettin to. Our maintenance people are out 365 days a year, an it's quite a job. When they're goin out into the hills they have full survival kits with them, an we monitor them very closely to check that they're safe.

DAVID LEE, *50, operations manager, Clunie power station,*
Pitlochry

We've got a string o power stations and associated works in the Tummel section – dams, gates, intakes and all the civil works, pipes an tunnels. An the extremes o weather ye get up there can cause problems. Heavy snow can cause problems, driftin into the aqueducts an chokin them. An Loch Ericht power station's on the south-east side o Loch Ericht, which runs from Rannoch up to Dalwhinnie, and ye can't get much remoter than that. But I tend to be drivin about to the power stations, rather than runnin about in the hills. I like the comforts of a car!

JOHN McDONALD, *32, maintenance engineer, Scottish*
Hydro Electric, Pitlochry

Many of Scotland's sixty-five towering hydro-electric dams can be seen from public roads, but the true scale of this modern engineering saga is hidden. There are hundreds of kilometres of rock tunnels, and massive excavations into rocky hillsides. The entirety of Glenmoriston power station near Loch Ness lies ninety metres underground, directly beneath the dam which feeds it.

And of all the magnates, inventors and entrepreneurs, the builders and destroyers who have restyled the terrain to their advantage, none have had the power over the landscape of the Hydro men.

We're responsible for a lot of the scenery in Scotland. A lot o the big lochs, we actually control the levels of. Ye can see a big difference.

JOHN McDONALD

If ye were goin through a drought the lochs wouldn't look very much, because they'd be low. But we keep a reasonable amount o water in them. We can move water from Loch Errochty into Loch Tummel, for example. An obviously the local people know it. But I think it's a measure of how successfully we're doin it that most people don't notice. They don't realise the abilities that we've got.

DAVID LEE

Not all the effects of this mastery of the elements are scenically fashionable, either. There are dry riverbeds and barren shorelines as the reservoirs empty to keep the generating turbines going. But the scheme which brought light to the margins is also now a business which turns over hundreds of millions of pounds, and exports electricity to England and Wales.

We get a lot of investors an suchlike goin through the power station. The big money people come through to have a look at what their money's doing. I'm kind of responsible for what they see, and ye take a kind of pride in the place. An the local kids come in, and I do like that. I have a much more sensible conversation wi them.

JOHN McDONALD

At 55 to 61 degrees North, Scotland is positioned just at the latitude where warm air from the equator meets cold air from the Arctic. The turbulence from this is what gives us such changeable, and often stormy, weather. The Borders shepherd and writer James Hogg recalled how Eskdalemuir, which in his time sustained 20,000 sheep, was left with just forty living lambs and five ewes by 'thirteen drifty days' of snow in the early seventeenth century. Floods are another local hazard; a day or two of unremitting rainfall after wet weather has already saturated the hillsides can drown villages and wipe out crops and stock. Over thirty centimetres of rain fell at Kinlochhourn on 5 and 6 February, 1989, and floods from the same storm swept away the railway bridge at Inverness.

We had one bad winter in, I think, '82, and I was stuck in the bus for eighteen hours with eleven of us in it between Tongue and Lairg. I had two passengers myself, and there was a lot o cars stuck, and they thought they'd be safer in the bus. It was terrible cold; I thought it was the end of everything. But the police found us with a probe, walking on top of the bus, and a helicopter took us out to Altnaharra. We were stuck there for three days. I was going to give up the job the next day, but I never did.

JOHN MACKAY, *61, postbus driver, Talmine*

We had a dry autumn last year, but we never, ever ran out of water. Ye don't run out of water in Scotland very often. An in a bad winter, when ye can have a lot of snow fallin, an runnin off, an heavy rain comin in, we generate very very heavily to try an make as much as we can. But our works fill up very quickly. We've managed small floods very well for years. But when ye get a major event – as happened in different parts in '89 and '90 and '93 . . . Well, I'm afraid our works can't really adequately help.

DAVID LEE

Let's just say I keep my map folded open at An Teallach. Fifty percent of our incidents come on or around that hill. It's a great attraction, because it's one of the finest ridge walks in the British Isles, but it has a particularily treacherous section where the highest number of fatalities are involved. And in general the more snow there is, the likelier that we'll have a fatality.

NEVIS HULME, *36, mountain rescue team leader and teacher, Gairloch*

Sunshine and rain can alternate through a day; on one May day in 1978 the temperature in Tummel Bridge varied from -7 to 22 degrees Centigrade. And though the hard-pressed farmers feel the most immediate brunt of any adversity, few areas of the country will pass many years without suffering the damage of flooding or high wind.

The hotel's built as a French chateau, with the gardens laid out in a formal style, what we used to call 'par terre'. Gardens are like everythin else, they're a sort o fashion statement. The seventeen an a half acres are laid out as the Capability Brown style of garden – the sweepin driveway towards the hotel, to keep ye in awe as ye get glimpses of the big buildin comin up the drive, an then the last twenty or thirty yards screened off until it hits ye. Really the garden was carved out of a moor, and one o the hardest things is, ye're right on top of a hillside, overlookin part of a glen, an the winds pound the gardens. It can be quite severe. An your hopes of growin things like camelias an that are just hopeless. But ye've got to be realistic about it.

LAWRENCE GORLAS, *40, head gardener, Gleneagles Hotel, Auchterarder*

I got a job here two years ago, and moved up from the north of England to a caravan in Durness. And I wouldn't like to say what the wind force is. I had two winters there, and they do the bombing things on Cape Wrath as well, so it was quite hectic.

JO MACKAY, *50, postbus driver, Durness*

Everythin for the Kelso ram sales is under canvas, about a mile of marquees, an they don't want the canvas standin up in the air too long, because of storms. So we're tested, to get all our pennin put up underneath the tents in time. A number of years ago there was a terrible gale on the Sunday night before the sales – seven or eight marquees torn to shreds, all matchwood everywhere, it was all gone. We were workin every hour God sent to put it back together.

WILLIAM DOUGLAS, *59, fencing contractor, Lilliesleaf*

But for all the perils and cruelties of a life on the land, nobody is more exposed to the dangerous whims of the Scottish climate than the mariners.

Ye know how the depressions come through the Northern Isles in the winter; ye can get a north-westerly gale going north, and coming south ye can get a south-easterly, so ye're gettin it the whole time, maybe for a week. The whole ship creaks and groans, and ye hear the water hittin the side; ye come off it like a zombie. It's not as bad as the old *St Clair*, though – she was particularly watery. You'd get waves comin down the funnel, it was quite spectacular.

DAVIE HIBBERT, *33, Chief Engineer,* St Sunniva

A Fine Job
THE COAST

Since the first currach brought our ancestors to these shores, sailors at sea were lucky to see the occasional hill-top beacon for guidance at night. But after a series of murderous storms in 1786 an expertise in the construction and operation of lighthouses was developed in Scotland (much of it by Robert Louis Stevenson's grandfather, uncle and father, who were successive Engineers to the Northern Lighthouse Board) and exported all over the world.

And, of course, there was a new breed of men living and working in novel conditions of hazard and isolation at the danger-spots round Scotland's 10,000 kilometres of coastline: the lighthouse keepers.

It's certainly a different way of life altogether. Ye've got time, and God made plenty of it, like. If ye don't like your ain company ye're in trouble. Them that's not fitted for it, I think the job kind of weeds them out along the way. They drop out in the early stages.

ERIC BRUCE, *50, assistant lightkeeper, Butt of Lewis lighthouse*

We have our moments, like. If ye're in the wrong place at the wrong time things do occur, and when ye're at the rock stations there's quite a bit of danger attached. There has been quite a number of lightkeepers lost over the years. At the Flannans, we used tae leave from East Loch Tarbert an head out in a ship an then put intae a launch in the lee of one o the islands. An one time durin a very bad gale we boarded the launch, an the seas were so terrible that we couldn't turn tae come intae the landin, so we were headin out intae the Atlantic. The ship was lookin for us, an the people on the island, an they couldn't see us. We were three hours, before they found us. But it's mainly yachts an things like that seem tae get intae difficulty. Another time at Rattray Head there was three or four men in a catamaran that capsized on a very dark wintry night – but we managed to save them all, an got the catamaran hauled up on the beach.

DONALD MICHAEL, 55, *principal lightkeeper, Butt of Lewis lighthouse*

Many legends are told of the men who have lived on these isolated frontiers, and there's no lightkeeper who isn't familiar with the story of the remote Flannan Islands light, which was found one winter's night in 1900, in perfect order, its clock stopped, a meal of cold meat, pickles and potatoes untouched on the kitchen table, and the crew vanished without trace.

But of all the bleak spots where the lights are kept burning, the thirty-seven metre redbrick tower of the Butt of Lewis lighthouse in the Outer Hebrides marks one of the most storm-tossed. Built in 1868, the tower was once named the windiest place in Britain by the *Guinness Book of Records*.

A keeper's main job is to make sure the navigation light is in proper operative condition in all weather. Even when it snows, ye've got tae clean the snow off the lantern with a broom, in gales or whatever, tae make sure the light can be seen from the sea.

DONALD MICHAEL

This is fairly the windiest place I've ever been at. It's very seldom ye get a still day. On Hogmanay night we had ninety-nine knots, an tryin to get your front door open an down the stairs – it's no that easy.

ERIC BRUCE

It was an engrained way of life for the right sort of men; 'the bee's knees,' as Second Assistant Lightkeeper John Drummond says. But Drummond was one of the last career lightkeepers recruited by the Northern Lighthouse Board, in 1973. By then it was clear that technology was going to wipe out this particular breed in a way the hurricanes never could.

One by one the manned lighthouses fell to automation. And long before it happened, the final deadline of 31 March, 1998 had become a date to chill the hearts of the last five crews. For what does an ex-lightkeeper do?

I've been movin round from lighthouse to lighthouse practically all my life, an findin somewhere tae settle down for the rest of your life is goin tae be hard. I'm very sad indeed.

DONALD MICHAEL

There may have been sound commercial reasons for the decision to automate the coastal lights, but the removal of the keepers from outposts where they were often an important part of tiny communities looks simply destructive today. Like all the coastal frontiersmen, they had learned the dangers of the elements, and risked them more than most.

I was workin the scaffy cart at the time – a refuse collector – an I was diggin the garden one day an the wife came out with this advert in the paper. Well, I thought, a lighthouse man. That would be a fine job. . . .

ERIC BRUCE

The Sea is Your Friend
and Your Enemy
THE OCEAN

More than the lighthouse men, more than the farmers, the hydro-electric maintenance crews, the drivers on the remote roads and the mountain rescuers, mariners today are the ones who live at the mercy of the elements. It's little wonder their attitude is ambivalent towards the bringer of both riches, and pain.

> The sea is your friend and your enemy. It'll show ye no mercy at times, and ye've got to draw a line between what's hardy and what's foolhardy in poor weather. She'll slap ye in the face very hardly. I've lost friends from the village at sea, and it shows; when tragedy strikes, it strikes everybody in the community.
> MICHAEL IAIN CURRIE, *34, trawler skipper, Mallaig*

This is one of the very last areas of our lives to retain a trace of the pagan gods, there in the water. For all our rational arguments and scientific understanding, the sea which has claimed the lives of so many from the coastal communities remains unfathomable and all-powerful. And like the boats with which the seamen wrestle the elements – it's a woman.

> Twelve years I've been with this boat. And ye get to know her moods and whims. There's a fine line between what ye can do with her, an what ye can't do with her.
> MICHAEL IAIN CURRIE

Growing up with estuary water at the foot of their street, or in sight of a wave-lashed harbour, the mariners have had the sea working its way into their lives from the earliest days. Whether merchant seamen on the far oceans, the crews of ferryboats plying the treacherous crossings, marine pilots guiding visiting vessels, or fishermen following the elusive shoals – generations have simply known that their destiny lay on the waters.

I had seafarin connections on both sides o the family. An I just never really thought of doin anythin else.

ALISTAIR MILLER, *59, Clyde pilot, Greenock*

I used to watch the fishing boats working at night in front of our house in Barra when I was a wee boy, working with herring an that, and I'd flash torches and try and attract their attention. It was always in my mind that that was what I wanted to do.

MICHAEL CURRIE, *46, lifeboat coxswain, Mallaig*

Ma grandfather was a Chief Engineer, an then ma father. An he took me away for a week when I was fifteen, an gave me tae the Mate an said: 'Gie him the dirtiest jobs.' That put me off for a while. But I still had a hankerin tae go tae sea.

DONALD CAMPBELL, *60, Clyde pilot, Greenock*

Nobody in Scotland is more than forty miles from the sea, and those who have made the water their highway and hunting-ground have the same sense of common tradition and inheritance as the families working the land. Nowhere is the feeling stronger than among the minority of fishermen who still run small family boats.

Fishing's something that's in the blood; all the family went to sea in one form or another. I'd work creels after school, and dodge school at times, and it was just a natural progression to making a life at sea. I arrived in Mallaig on my sixteenth birthday, and went out with Michael in the boat for a week. And I stayed nineteen years.

MICHAEL IAIN CURRIE

I left school on the Friday, and on the Monday I joined the *Margaret Sinclair*, the boat that my father was on. Then after two years an a spell deep-sea I came up to Mallaig and got a job on a creel boat for lobster-fishing, the *Isabella*, an then another boat, the *Excellent the Third*, and then I went trawling whitefish in the Atlantic. In 1974 I managed to get enough together for a deposit on a boat of my own, and got my Class 2 certificate in Aberdeen, so I was a skipper. And after about six years I bought the *Valiant of Fraserburgh*, and renamed her the *Five Sisters*, after my five daughters.

MICHAEL CURRIE

The tradition persists, but this is a generation whose inheritance at sea is far from secure. Mallaig trawler-owner Michael Currie himself is one of those who have felt the old ways slipping away, and taken a step back. While he makes his life closer to shore, it is the brother he shares a name with (in the tradition of their birthplace, the island of Barra), who continues the captaincy of the *Five Sisters*.

Little more than twenty years ago, it was herring which Mallaig's boats were bringing in to the remote west-coast village. The port had been famed since the days when the Scottish fleet and its following army of 'fisher lasses' trailed the dense shoals around the coast, building a huge trade with the Continent, pre-Revolutionary Russia and the Baltic States.

But when international over-fishing finally outpaced the customs of centuries in the late 1970s, herring fishing was banned for several years, and stocks are still patchy. The emphasis today is on mackerel, most of which are 'klondyked' – transferred from fishing boats to the looming, clanking factory ships of (mainly foreign) buyers.

> I was trawling whitefish for three years, and when the weather was bad we used to labour on the Norwegian klondykers, shovelling boxes of ice; the money was good then.
>
> MICHAEL CURRIE

Alternative seafoods have become more popular, too, like the nephrops or Norway lobster, whose tails are used for scampi. The fishermen who sail the unpredictable waters of the Minches between Mallaig and Stornoway call them 'prawns'.

> Aye, prawn fishing is a delicate subject. On Sunday night ye make your plans for Monday morning, and ye can be on grounds that have an abundance o prawns one week, an the next week there's nothing. The frustration is being in the right place at the right time. Sometimes ye'd work a thirty-six hour shift without stoppin if the fishing was good; the crew are sleeping while ye're doing the first trawl, and then they work that catch while you go to sleep.
>
> MICHAEL CURRIE

> When ye get a good catch, that's the best part of it. Ye know yourself, the minute ye haul, if it's a good one.
>
> ARCHIE DEMPSTER, *brother-in-law of the Curries, 29,*
> *trawlerman, Mallaig*

Ye're up from peep o dawn to crack o night. And ye're living with each other five days of the week, so ye have to get on well. If the fishing's slack, we'll be Monday right through to the following Thursday.

MICHAEL IAIN CURRIE

I like the *Five Sisters*, it's an easy boat to work. And for me – I love prawns. I could live on them. Sometimes we eat them here on the boat, but I take a bag of them home myself every weekend. I love them!

ARCHIE DEMPSTER

By tradition Scots fishermen work a 'share crew' system which divides the profits of a vessel's earnings. If there are profits. These small businessmen in unfashionably small boats are competing with international fleets which have little time for sentimentality, and also with European political pressures (always tending to shrink the Scottish fleet and fish quotas) which seem far beyond any sort of local influence.

So now the men who live their lives in balance with the dangerous and uniquely changeable Scottish seas all year turn their weather eye to Brussels for the storm which will carry them off.

Some weeks ye would go without a wage, and some weeks ye would get a good wage. But the hours ye had to put in was something else. In the middle o summer ye worked the daylight hours, three or four in the morning till eleven at night. And once ye've sorted the fish ye'd put the boat to broadside and lie out just to get two or three hours' sleep. Basically ye've got to be at sea twenty-four hours a day, seven days a week, and that's the only way ye could make it pay.

MICHAEL CURRIE

Mallaig is very much a fishing community; if there's no fish, there's no money in the village. And it's changed a lot over the years. The boats have got more an the fish have got less, and every year it gets that bitty more difficult. And it's painful to see boats pulled up on the beach and struck from their glory – a man's pride and joy at one time, and they're just hulks.

MICHAEL IAIN CURRIE

Ye're Stinkin!
FISH PROCESSORS

There's no better illustration of how things have changed in the fishing business than Peterhead. Far from the struggles of the small fishing settlements, this north-east town has grown to become Europe's biggest fishing port, serving fleets of big ships from most of the countries on the continent. Landings by foreign vessels in Scottish ports grew from around 2,800,000 in 1984 to more than 20 million ten years later. And life at the hub of the international industry is a very far cry from the social and craft traditions which tied folk to the sea for so many generations.

When the signatures are scrawled and the handshakes exchanged, most of the catch here is bound for the fish processing industry which has grown up around Peterhead harbour. And here it's grim work. The herring girls on the quayside, dazzlingly nimble with the razor-sharp filleting knife, have been replaced by the churning clatter of automated machinery.

I'm workin machines maistly, pittin fish along a belt an mak sure they're goin through the right way an nothin's gettin stuck. It is borin, waitin tae get a break an thinkin about eight o'clock in the mornin, an ye canna hear the radio for the machines. But some o us have personal stereos, like, an that passes the night. We swap tapes, an I'll listen tae onythin, I'm no fussy. But I've no got mines the night, I'm just havin a yap, like.

JENNY McCONNELL, *18, machine operator, Peterhead*

It's a long shift, shiftin boxes an stackin pallets an loadin lorries, an ye're comin out in the dark an goin home in the dark, so it's pretty weird.

GAVIN KELLY, *21, general labourer, Peterhead*

Naw, it's spot-on for me. I came tae the fish straight fae school, an I like a night-shift, like, it's just fine nae havin tae get up in the mornins. An it seems like a long weekend;

ye finish on Saturday mornin, an ye get the hale o Monday off till eight o'clock.

JENNY McCONNELL

At the peak seasons for mackerel (October to March) and herring (June to October), the processors hire extra hands to keep the machines turning through the night. Occasionally there are slack moments, waiting for the vessels to come in, but for the mostly-young operators who do this poorly paid, repetitive work on twelve-hour shifts, 'the crack' is what makes it tolerable.

I don't particularily like workin wi the fish. But wi the people here ye get a good laugh, an that's what makes the difference. An sometimes ye get a wee break waitin for the fish to come in, have a cup o tea an a crack an a game of cards in the canteen. And ye might get a chat wi the lorry-drivers when they come in. Some o them go over tae Brittany an that, an further.

GAVIN KELLY

I think ma mum would like me tae have a better job, but I'm goin tae be here till I decide fit I want tae do. But she's murder about the smell! 'Get those clothes off, ye're stinkin!'

JENNY McCONNELL

It does smell when ye first come in here – but the money disnae smell, like, an that's what counts.

GAVIN KELLY

It's Hard Nowadays for
Any Youngsters
PILOTS AND FERRYMEN

Once the hundreds of thousands of tonnes of fresh catch at Peterhead are graded and filleted, skinned or marinated or frozen, they might be destined for the Far East, straight back out of the harbour in refrigerated bulk vessel, or perhaps mackerel by container lorry to the Scandinavian countries, where they will be smoked. Small fish often go to Taiwan or Korea, to be used as bait in catching swordfish or tuna.

And any fish which is reloaded onto a cargo vessel for shipment to foreign parts may instantly find itself in the hands of a seafarer who's well acquainted with its far-flung destination – because all boats over sixty metres are legally bound to be guided through coastal waters by a local pilot. Like most of Scotland's merchant seamen and many of the fishermen, these are men who have sailed 'deep-sea' from ports all over the world in their youth. And there's something in the tales they have to tell, a sense of foreign adventure, which makes a connection all the way back to the earliest explorers.

I went tae sea wi the Donaldson Line at eighteen, in the Atlantic an South America, an runnin emigrants tae New Zealand. At twenty-seven I got ma Master's certificate, an our company was dead men's shoes, workin your way up. Then I was in a wee ship runnin tae Nova Scotia in the winter-time, eighteen days tae get there, an it wasnae very nice. The chief engineer used tae sleep in his bath. So I put in for the pilotage.

DONALD CAMPBELL, 60, *Clyde pilot, Greenock*

I went worldwide as a junior engineer, the South Pacific an New Caledonia. An then in the early '80s I worked for a company in Liberia, in Africa. This was the second biggest shippin line in the world, but the company was a bit poor. Well, on the verge of bankruptcy. An we started gettin a bit short o food, an runnin out o fuel, an things like that. So that was a bit grim. In the end I came back to Scotland, an did ma Class 2 certificate in Aberdeen.

DAVIE HIBBERT, *33, chief engineer,* St Sunniva

I grew up in Plockton with a bit of sailing and fishing, and joined a Liverpool line as a cadet when I was seventeen. I was in Saudi Arabia, and then the Middle East as a pilot for a couple of years, and then Bahrain, and then for my sins I was harbourmaster at Kyle of Lochalsh for two years. Then to Papua, New Guinea, but the natives were gettin restless – the last of the boat people were a pretty angry bunch with big knives and things like that – and then I came onto the Clyde. And anywhere that doesn't dump 30,000 tonnes of water on your head every day like the west coast of Scotland has to be looked on favourably, but I've got family commitments here. So I won't be doing any more rovin for some time.

DOUGLAS MACKENZIE, 47, *Clyde pilot, Greenock*

Many of the seafarers are still out there, somewhere in the wide blue yonder. A fair few of them in the past ended up as smugglers and pirates, and no doubt a fair few of them still are.

But among those who do return, the pilotage is a job of some standing. Every pilot is a Master Mariner, but the breadth of his international experience is matched by his intimate local knowledge of his patch. In an area like the Clyde estuary – over 1000 square kilometres of river, firth and neighbouring sea-lochs – he'll know every detail of the tide, swell and current at any time of the day or night; every small feature in the undersea landscape, every possible eccentricity in the weather, and how each factor will affect the handling of ships which range from empty cargo boats to towering passenger liners.

Ye do four years' trainin, startin out on small ships and gradually workin your way up till ye're full tonnage an they let ye loose on supertankers. That's completely different from anythin else; we've had 350,000 tonnes in at Finnart, and ye have tae think very far ahead – they take three miles tae stop, an by the time we're gettin up tae the berth we've got two tugs on them actin as brakes.

DONALD CAMPBELL

Ye keep it all in your head – the physical limits of the estuary, the Gantock Rocks that ye have to avoid, an shallow patches at Skelmorlie Bank; ye seldom need to consult charts. An ye're always conscious of the weather and other traffic. The estuary is vastly used by commercial traffic an naval vessels, an by yachtsmen in the summer, and ye have to be aware of them, particularily if they're racin. Sometimes they seem to get excited, and they don't seem to be completely aware of what else is going on in the river.

ALISTAIR MILLER, *59, Clyde pilot, Greenock*

When he is on call, a pilot can be summoned to his port at any hour. Often he will find himself taking a pilot cutter in poor conditions to meet a ship which he will have to board by literally jumping onto a ladder at its side. And once he reaches the bridge, the real work of handling the boat and its captain begins.

Oh yes, it's quite hazardous. When you're transferring from the pilot cutter to an incoming ship on a winter's night in the dark and a long way to climb, you can't go up and check the ladder's made fast. We've had three pilots in the water during my time on the estuary.

ALISTAIR MILLER

Ye certainly see a lot of white knuckles in this business – sometimes mine. Ye're dealin with big lumps of metal and human elements, and it can create its own adrenalin. Once ye take a ship up the river it's all very narrow, and that combined with a strong tide and cross winds and ye've got to be a wee bit on the ball.

DOUGLAS MACKENZIE

If ye're pilotin somebody from Cumbrae to Glasgow ye'll be with them for five hours or so. But I've met dozens of nationalities, an I could count the bad rascals probably on the fingers of one hand.

ALISTAIR MILLER

Typically, our coastal traffic has changed almost out of recognition even in the time the pilots have been at sea. Not so long ago the

Clyde bustled with handsome ferry-boats taking trippers 'doon the watter' to a world of Victorian piers at the resorts of the estuary and beyond. Then there were the shoals of little steam 'puffers' which carried cargoes of all the essentials to the islands and communities of the west coast. This was a picturesque trade – celebrated in Neil Munro's Para Handy stories and screen offspring like the film *The Maggie* – which bred its own mythology.

> You can tell the girls of Arran, you can tell the girls of Troon,
> You can tell the girls of Rothesay that I'll be coming soon.
> All the nice girls love a sailor, so it's me that gets the vote,
> I'm the mate, the cook and fireman of a shore-heid boat!
> from 'Shore-heid Boat' by Ian Philip

> We've got our own pier down the bay here, an everythin used to come in to the distillery by boat until about '84.
> ANDY MacDONALD, *31, production manager, Talisker distillery, Carbost*

Today, ninety percent of goods in Scotland reach their destination by road (and most people, too). And it's not just the excursion boats and the puffers which have been put out of business by the policy-makers' determination to favour four-wheeled transport. Containerisation has vastly increased the amount of cargo leaving Scotland on lorries bound for the south of England, at the expense of the Scottish ports' bulk business.

> When they started puttin things in boxes, that was the demise of the traffic on the river.
> DONALD CAMPBELL

> When Donald an I started, ye didnae get in to the pilotage till ye were thirty, an if ye weren't in by thirty-five, ye didnae get in. The retirees weren't replaced over the years, an it's probably kept a livin goin for the fewer an fewer that remain; but in a very few years all the pilots could be gone.
> ALISTAIR MILLER

A life on Scotland's waters is no longer something a boy can be born to. There simply isn't the work, even on the boats that remain. Just as the foreign 'quota-hoppers' can buy up Scottish fishing boats to exploit the flag's entitlement to a share of fish, much of the British merchant fleet is now crewed by foreigners working under a flag of convenience.

> It's hard nowadays for any youngsters with the sea in their blood, the merchant navy bein the way it is.
>
> ALISTAIR MILLER

Brussels, and Westminster, and the big boys of international fishing and shipping, have put on the squeeze. But there's one steady prospect still there for some of the seamen – at least as long as the bridge-builders keep off the bulk of our 130 inhabited islands. More than a few sea-dogs who might be remembered for one reason or another in Halifax or Hamburg or Hong Kong can be found today in the mess-room of a ferry making its daily return crossing from the Scottish mainland.

These are the lifeline services, the dotted lines on tourist maps, linking the outposts to the mainland at Oban and Mallaig, Aberdeen, Ardrossan, Tarbert, Ullapool, Scrabster. The companies which run them draw millions of pounds in subsidies to maintain the links with the outlying places. And for many of the seamen, like Captain William James Duncan of the 400-passenger *St Sunniva* and most of his crew, the ferries are what made it possible to come home.

> When I joined the *St Ola* ten years ago, ye did feel a wee bit more claustrophobic after bein away. Ye didnae seem to have so much time on your own. But some o the crew, we'd done deep-sea together, so that helped. An now, the *Sunniva*'s the best out o the three boats. The crew are excellent; there's never any arguments. Everybody's easy-ozy. An I've got three young children, an this is a lot better than bein away eight or nine months. They ken fine they'll be round the local sweetie-shop as soon as ye're back. An they've come through and visited the boat, like. They just think it's magic; they're only used to seein small fishin boats, and when they see a thing like this – it's just ginormous!
>
> ALEXANDER COULL, 37, *bosun,* St Sunniva

> Ye're not goin anywhere very interestin, but I'm quite glad to be away from deep-sea. Ye spent so little time in port, it

was a waste of time. Ye could watch the world goin past with binoculars, and that was about it.

DAVIE HIBBERT

The main cargo is for the farms – livestock feed an tractors, an livestock itself. The *Sunniva* is the main link to the mainland, so ye get to know the regulars travellin backwards and forwards. They're awful friendly.

ALEXANDER COULL

William Duncan was originally a fisherman from Lossiemouth, and worked his way up the merchant navy ranks until he became Master of the *Sunniva* in 1987. And the boat's 190-mile journey between Aberdeen and Lerwick takes her through seas which can present hazards to match anywhere in the world. The Pentland Firth, between the north coast and Orkney, is a busy international shipping channel which has the fastest-flowing currents in Europe and a range of riptides, whirlpools and skerries with their own names and stories – the Merry Men O Mey, the Western Bore, the Swelkie.

The wreck of the first *St Sunniva* can still be seen on the east coast of the Shetland island of Mousa, where it ran aground in thick fog in 1930; and the current ship had no gentle introduction to the local conditions. Her bridge windows were smashed in by twenty-metre waves on her maiden trip.

We can get fairly rough weather. It has its moments. But if it gets too bad, we just delay the sailin. When the wind's south-easterly, that's the worst for us. Once ye're lookin at thirty-five to forty knots, ye have to think very carefully.

CAPTAIN WILLIAM JAMES DUNCAN, 51, master,
St Sunniva

Talking to most of them, you get the impression that these are men who rarely dwell on the rhythms which link them to the waters – the swell underfoot, the harbour receding behind and the horizon opening up in front, the ways of generations before them, the familiar faces, the beat of the engine. As they say themselves, it's in their blood. But the truth is that with technology and international politics and bureaucracy and commerce closing in, these are the voices of a shrinking band; the last of the Scottish mariners.

The *Sunniva* is an excellent ship – very sea-kindly an safe; manoeuvrable. She's got a good feelin about her. At the weekends we do mini-cruises for passengers, an weather permitting we go down past the Old Man of Hoy, and Marwick Head, the Kitchener's memorial, an Rousay Sound with the seabird colonies. Sumburgh Head, an ye go a wee bit closer to let them see the rock formations. And ye never get stale with it. Ye never get stale. Ye see somethin different every time.

WILLIAM DUNCAN

When haddocks leave the Firth of Forth,
And mussels leave the shore,
When oysters climb up Berwick Law,
We'll go to sea no more,
No more, We'll go to sea no more.

'The Fisherman's Song', from Norah and William
Montgomerie's *Scottish Nursery Rhymes*

Having Seen it All Before
CROFTERS AND LANDOWNERS

Among the life-shaping policies which are passed out to the edge from a distant centre, it's a curious aspect of the way the Common Agricultural Policy has worked that the bigger a Scottish farm, the more profitable is its subsidy. The people who pull the strings have managed to discriminate, as if by chance, against the little men. And of course the 'little men' of Scottish agriculture, following the same family respect for tradition and waging the same battle with unforgiving nature as the fisherman with his boat or the farmer with all his tractors and combines and computerised equipment, are the crofters.

> If ye've got a croft ye've got to work at it, and it's all go, really. I've just been haulin home hay, and it gets dark an that forces ye to sit down. But there's always fences to pitch or sheep to chase.
>
> MALCOLM MACDONALD, *53, crofter, Glendale, Skye*

There's no better example than this, of thrawn persistence in bleak surroundings. Shunted to the poorest land on the margins of the wealthy estates by eighteenth or nineteenth-century landowners who had discovered that sheep pasture or grouse moors brought in more money than tenants, the crofters are still there. On the shores and the hard ground of the seven crofting counties round north Scotland's edge – Argyll, Inverness, Ross and Cromarty, Sutherland, Caithness, Orkney and Shetland – are some 17,500 crofts, averaging just a handful of acres each.

And though these smallholders are every bit as vital to local communities as the farmers (crofting families account for some eighty percent of the population of the Western Isles) they are used to having to get by without the safety-net of huge subsidies. Given the limitations of their tiny plots of land, the crofters have always simply had to forge links with other areas of business just to survive.

When I got a job with the Forestry in 1975 it was just goin full swing, it was very good. They were buyin a lot o new ground, and fencin, drainin, ploughin and plantin. There was no shortage of work. It was great. There was a squad in each area, for goodness' sake – Dunvegan, Portree, Raasay and Elgol. And the type o people employed were all more or less the same background and the same mind. People got on really well together. And most of the foresters then came up through the ranks – they started off workin wi the squad, and went to college. It was good, it really was.

MALCOLM MacDONALD

Near the coasts, a crofter might also be a fisherman, or gather seaweed for animal feed. A crofting family today might have an interest in a fish farm, or the bed-and-breakfast trade. And the work which sustained Malcolm MacDonald on his croft on the island of Skye is part of the national reforestation which has been going on since the Great War. Thousands of years after the Caledonian Forest was hacked away, it's not pine and birch which loom over us, but everywhere a landscape dressed in sought-after North American sitka spruce. Like the farming business, the conditions of life here have depended on decisions made far away; but for many in the Highlands, the work has been good.

In 1964 there were fourteen of us in a squad in North Strome forest, cutting wood on the shores of Loch Carron for the new pulp mill at Corpach, and there was a lot of well-educated people. We had an ex-RSM workin with us, and the discussions . . . The conversation was good. Then that wind blew in Argyll. There was a fearful tonnage of wood down, and they cut back on tree-cutting in the north to get the wood cleared. I moved more into maintenance; the Forestry owned a lot of houses, and we travelled round reshingling them.

ALASDAIR MACKENZIE, 55, *forester, Loch Carron*

In little more than two generations the landscape has been transformed. And in areas where the trees are coming to maturity, there are new opportunities for the crofting communities.

I left school at sixteen and worked on the croft – my father had it before me – and various odd jobs here and there. There were only two Forestry Commission workers on Raasay, my

father and my uncle, and when my uncle retired, I applied for
the job – not necessarily out o choosin forestry as a career,
but more the scarcity of employment on the island. My father
worked for another three years, an then it was just me on my
own. An it was pretty hopeless, really. Some jobs ye don't
really mind if ye're on your own or not; out on the hills at
lambin time ye don't really miss company. But if ye're in the
wood on your own, ye get gey fed up wi it. But I stuck it out.
And it's certainly lookin up now. They've started extractin
timber, and puttin in bridges an culverts an things for the
harvestin machinery. A few years ago Raasay was a great
problem to them from the point o view o gettin timber out
o the place, but they're introducin barges to take the wood
away. And it's grand to see some activity.

MALCOLM MACKAY, *38, forester, Raasay*

The spread of the trees is still going on, and even though it's much
slower than thirty years ago, the annual loss of agricultural land to
forestry in Scotland is still substantially more than the combined
encroachment of roads, mineral workings, industry, recreational
facilities and housing. But the huge plantings are finished; the
heyday of the forester is over. Most of the jobs which had been
promised to bring local prosperity have gone, and much of the
remaining work, like the forests themselves, is being offloaded
to outside companies with variable hiring policies. There is an
uncertain future in the woods.

It's all gone now. It's whittled down to almost nothin, and
the little that is done is goin out to contractors, like every
other job nowadays. There's only a few of us left on Skye;
four out o five that was in the south end have gone, and I'm
a ganger, in charge of a squad, if ye can call it that – there's
six of us left here. People are so unsettled with not knowin
what's round the corner. It's sad in a way. But it's the same
all over.

MALCOLM MacDONALD

I'm Loch Carron born and bred, and my grandfather built
this house in 1896. The family crofted there before me as far
back as I know. And the forestry certainly went well with
croftin communities, years ago. But there's more machinery
now, and contractors, and from this weekend I'll be on my

own – the chap that's workin with me is takin redundancy. I'd like to retire when I'm sixty, and just concentrate on lookin after the croft – five acres, and just a few sheep.

ALASDAIR MACKENZIE

It was just the ideal job for people who had crofts. The pay wasn't great, but ye had an income, and it allowed ye to do your croft at the same time, where ye couldn't live off either. We've got croftin goin back generations in the family, but I don't know how long it's goin to last now. That's the unfortunate thing.

MALCOLM MacDONALD

There's some bitterness at how the forestry business has turned out in Scotland. Most of the work it provided has gone, and after the sheep, the deer and game birds, trees look very much like another way of clearing people off the land for somebody else's profit. The unsettling thing is, it doesn't take much for the archaeologists to paint a picture of how lively this landscape once was, when it was home to the people who first toiled to clear the trees, level the ground, build the dykes and hedges.

The whole of Highland Region is extremely rich in archaeo-logical monuments. In a broad swathe three-and-a-half kilo-metres by three hundred metres we've found seven hundred sites which are man-made; and I don't think that's untypical of areas of farmland in Scotland.

ROD McCULLAGH, 39, *archaeologist, Achany Glen*

The quantity of archaeological riches in an area which is poor by most normal standards may seem strange to anyone who's unfamiliar with the way the Highlands have been managed for the last three centuries. But the unhappy truth is that the same forces which cleared away the people have preserved the past in a way which the busy lowland ploughs would never have permitted.

And it's not a happy thing to realise that the ones pulling the strings here are very often the descendants of the landlords who first enforced the Clearances two hundred and fifty years ago. Today around about six hundred people own half of Scotland. But the problem is not the fact of a roomful of folk owning a vast amount of the land, it's the extraordinary powers they've managed to hold onto, and the way they can still abuse them.

PROFIT-HUNGRY LAIRD PLANS
'DEESIDE CLEARANCE'

A Scots laird is refusing to listen to the entreaties of a community fearful that his plan to evict twenty families from his estate will rip the heart out of their village.

John Foster, a landowner who also has an estate at Leuchars, plans to remove tenants from their homes so he can sell a large slice of the 200,000-acre Park Estate, near the Deeside village of Drumoak.

The first evictions in what has become known as the 'Deeside Clearance' will take place within a fortnight. Most of the tenants involved have lived in their basic, spartan cottages for upwards of a decade; one family has been there for twenty-five years.

Scotland on Sunday, 16 March, 1997

If much of Scotland seems strangely preserved in the same wilderness state as at the height of society tourism more than a hundred years ago (Queen Victoria bought Balmoral Castle in 1852) it's easier to understand when you know that the land law, too, has been embalmed. Evictions, obscure 'reversions' of private properties to estate ownership, the denial of rights of way to walkers – this is the way of it on Scottish land today, while millions of acres of the Highlands are kept desolate for the occasional sporting outing by a small number of rich people who generally don't even live in this country.

The misuse of landowning power is all the harder to bear, too, because it runs directly against a fierce popular tradition of freedom of the land.

> For years we've been encouragin people to get out on the hills an make use o them. An they've taken us at our word. The whole scene has changed. The numbers are much greater, an there's more an more problems on the hills, an more pressure. But there's no real criticism o the people who need rescued; it's somethin that can happen to any of us. There's a strong tradition in this country of people bein free to go on the hills, an if they have problems they won't be penalised for it.
>
> JIM BUCHANAN, 41, *mountain rescue team equipment officer, Dundonnell*

It was civil unrest, particularly in Skye (where Westminster sent a gunboat and troops in the early 1880s) which resulted in the one substantial inroad into the feudal land law, the Crofter's Act of 1886. Since this time, crofters have had security of tenure at reasonable rents. And in recent years it has been the crofting communities once more which have taken the initiative against inadequate landlords.

In 1992 the 130 men and women of the Assynt Crofters' Trust took possession of a 21,000 acre estate in Sutherland from the receivers of a bankrupt Swedish property company with a simple and powerful statement of intent.

> We the crofters have resolved to band together to buy the estate, not for reasons motivated by political or romantic sentiment but because we believe that to give our crofting communities the best chance of surviving in the future, control of resources – especially the land – will be our best chance.
>
> *Assynt Crofters' Trust Fund Appeal*, 28 July, 1992

In 1993, with grants and loans and money they had raised themselves, the tenants of Assynt bought their land for £300,000.

> There is a thing in the Highlands which is to do with people having seen it all before – a desire to let other people do it, because they're the ones that want to do it. A desire not to put yourself forward. But they were goin to split the estate up into lots of wee tiny bits, and it was offered for sale in a shiny brochure, and we had a group of influential an powerful people, a mixture of local people an incomers, who kind of fired people up. I think the time was right, and we had good leaders. And it was absolutely bloody magic when we made it. We were in the school in Stoer, there must have been a hundred people there, and somebody brought in the lawyer, and a huge cheer went up. And there was this wonderful, overwhelming sense of euphoria that we'd accomplished it. I've never experienced anything like that, that just embraced everybody, 100 percent.
>
> AILEEN KINNAIRD, 47, *teacher, Lochinver*

Assynt became a famous symbol of what was possible on Scottish land, and created a mood for change. Recently the government began the first moves to transfer crofting land which they had bought for resettlement in the early part of the century into the ownership of the 1362 tenant crofters themselves. In the mid-1990s the 200-strong Highland community of Laggan negotiated itself into partnership with the Forestry Commission, setting up a plan which will see local people taking the jobs and guiding the management decisions of a 3000-acre forest. The first thirty-eight-tonne load of newly felled timber from Strathmashie Forest was hauled to the mill in early 1998. And more will follow the Laggan pioneers.

But new and powerful outside interests are beginning to make their mark on Scottish land ownership, too. Assynt was bought with the help of £20,000 from Scottish Natural Heritage. And in April 1997 the island of Eigg, which had suffered under a series of foreign and absentee owners, was finally purchased by a consortium including the sixty-eight islanders and Highland Council. The third partner in the consortium, Scottish Wildlife Trust, is a sign of the way things are going in the 'wilderness'. After 8000 years of changing the place around, the new lairds are conservationists. . . .

Deeper Feelings
THE ENVIRONMENTAL AGENDA

The campaign for the natural world is a relatively new phenomenon. It has crept over us with new ideas, and new jargon. The word 'conservation' itself only came into general use in the 1970s, and now we have 'biodiversity' (the number of species), 'sustainability' (the degree to which any activity is self-supported without environmental damage), the 'agri-environment' (farmland, as it happens) and all the rest.

Odd, you might say, to spend all of history moving the furniture around to suit ourselves, and then thirty years trying to preserve it as it stands. But this modern sense that people are doing damage to the world has started an awful lot of fights. Spouting moral principles with the enthusiasm of religious converts, environmental campaigners come up against every sort of commercial interest, many old-fashioned ways of viewing the world, many progressive social ideas, and, often, each other.

Questions to do with what we make of the world around us don't just polarise conflicting organisations, either. They can change people's attitudes to the place they live in, when the prospect of new wealth turns up, and split communities.

> Ye'll notice the change more in the incomers, even people who have been here forty or fifty years, than ye'd notice it in the native island people whose roots really are embedded in the rock of the island. But even families are divided over whether they want the superquarry. Ye'll get maybe a husband who looks favourably on it, and the wife an the rest of the family are against it, or vice-versa. And it's affected the community that way.
>
> JOHN MACAULAY, 56, Flodabay, Harris

The good news – and the bad news – is that Scotland has plenty of fertile ground for this sort of dispute. The geological pedigree which makes for bleak farmland has given us a treasure-trove beneath the soil. Rubislaw quarry in the west of Aberdeen, disgorging 60,000 tonnes of granite a year at the turn of the century, became the second-biggest man-made hole in the planet (after one of the South African diamond mines). And in the 1990s we've had to take on board the idea of a 'superquarry' on Harris, in the Outer Hebrides, which would render one of Scotland's most beautiful landscapes into the foundation rubble for a hundred European super-roads.

> There was quite a large quarry at Lingerbay during the war, but that shut down, and there was quite serious unemployment. So there was always the hope that it would be revived in some way, and various attempts were made. And when this came up, and people realised it was a big company, and not just another story, they were very hopeful at the prospects of long-term employment starting up again. But after a relatively short period of time, when people were looking into this new idea, a superquarry, maybe the biggest about in the world – they began to think it would be too big for Harris. That it would completely overwhelm the island.
>
> JOHN MACAULAY

Here's a place of remote beauty, in desperate need of jobs and money. Something like twenty-five environmental groups opposed the quarry, and during years of soul-searching and campaigning, the islanders have voted both for and against the development in successive referenda. By 1997, the developers were offering them £12 million to change their minds – a sum amounting, as one unimpressed islander pointed out, to £100 a year for each of them during the sixty-year life of the quarry.

In the meantime the conservationists, too, have been advancing. A fifth of Scotland is now covered by a boggling selection of woolly green labels: Local Nature Reserve, Site of Special Scientific Interest, Environmentally Sensitive Areas, National Scenic Areas, Regional Parks. . . . The environmental agenda goes much deeper than titles, too.

RESERVED STOCKS
The past year has seen startling progress on reserve ownership, with, on one occasion, over 50 negotiations in progress at once!

> . . .Buying land is an urgent task and one which
> is well supported by our members through Appeals.
> *Scottish Wildlife Trust Annual Review, 1992-93*

Environmental groups own hundreds of thousands of acres of
Scotland, and their estate is growing by the day as they push
to gain control of everything they want to protect. Islands which
were despairingly abandoned by their native communities within
living memory, are now owned, and often populated, by the conservationists (St Kilda, the National Trust for Scotland; Isle Martin, the
RSPB; Canna, NTS; Rum, Scottish National Heritage, and so on).

Yet on the small scale, community involvement, consultation
and partnership often does seem to work, with conservation guaran-
teed as one of the main ingredients of the mix. The Montrose
tidal basin on the Angus coast is an area exceptionally rich in
birdlife, with populations of eider ducks, redshank and greylag
geese. A large proportion of the world's pinkfooted geese come
every year, as well, and many locals have got used to mapping
their own year by the onset of winter in distant Iceland and
Greenland.

I love to see an hear the first geese every year. It's always the
week after September the tenth. When we were old enough,
a friend an I would be up at five o'clock, cycle to the Basin
with a gun strapped to our backs, an a two-mile walk to wait
for the geese to flight at the first crack o dawn. Hopefully,
we'd be in the right place to get in a shot when they'd start
to take off from the roostin ground. At that time, Montrose
Basin was very much an anythin-goes job. Some mornins it
was quite possible to see more wildfowlers than geese. An as
the roads from the south got better, we were gettin more and
more visitors from south o the Border comin up to shoot,
an between one thing an another the geese got absolutely
no peace. An consequently the number was declining. Well,
Montrose Wildfowlers, the local wildfowling club, realised
the pressures on the geese, an how precious a place that
was. An they attempted to make it a nature reserve. But
they had no clout. They'd had the seeds of an idea, but no
method of putting it forward. An frankly, nobody else was
bothered.

IAN MONTGOMERIE, *43, PE teacher, Montrose*

In the end it was the Scottish Wildlife Trust – the country's biggest voluntary wildlife conservation body, with 10,000 members – who bothered. Of all the environmental bodies, the SWT have set the pace by showing themselves willing to share power and responsibility in areas such as the Montrose Basin and Eigg.

Montrose Basin is now managed as a Local Nature Reserve in partnership with the local council and neighbouring landowners, and consultation with people who live in the area. The bulk of the reserve is owned by SWT, and the rest by farmers and landowners who volunteered to join the arrangement. There are shooting permits for 100 locals, and five-day permits for a limited number of visitors.

> The locals were very sceptical at first. We suddenly heard that it had been bought by the Wildlife Trust, an there was pure panic. But we had a voice on the management committee; most of our ideas were taken on board; an it was reassuring how they were speakin to us. And we have a mutual respect now. There's no doubt that the reserve wouldn't work without cooperation. An my personal feelin is that if we hadn't had this reserve, an the restrictions, an the permits, an the rest of it, the Montrose Basin would've been finished as a conservation area long ago. An now it's more enjoyable. Because even if ye don't get a shot, ye will always see a lot o geese pourin into the place. One o the last times I was out, there must've been twenty or thirty thousand. The sky was black wi them in the evening flight. Quite an impressive sight. Quite a movin sight.
>
> IAN MONTGOMERIE

The ranger/naturalist at Montrose Basin is the link between the different points of view on the issues. Rick Goater came to Montrose in 1986 with responsibility for dealing with all the conflicting interests at the site, organising local volunteers to help with things like litter sweeps and hide-building, seeing the local bye-laws are kept, and lecturing to groups in the community.

> I live on the edge of the Basin, and every time the geese come past I can't help but rush out and look. They come in with the lines wavering and reforming, quite high over my house, and then suddenly all the lines crack up and become a bee-swarm

shape plummeting down, twisting and turning, and it's just a magnificent sight. It sounds like a train or something, a great rushing noise. Wiffling, it's called. A lot of the wildfowlers years ago got that sort of magical feeling from geese, they'd be quite happy to go out and not shoot anything. It was the morning flight, and the sound, and the cold, and that kind of thing. But it's quite a sharp division at the Basin now. Most day-passes are used up by quite wealthy people from the south of England, and they can't say enough in praise of geese, and the adrenalin and the excitement, and the one week a year they get away to dear old Scotland, and all that sort of thing. The local people, they've shot all their lives, their dads did it before them, and they're much more, almost, military. It's camouflage gear and black balaclavas, and I don't like that really. Because I sense they're doing it without any deeper feelings for the geese.

RICK GOATER, *38, ranger/naturalist, Montrose Basin*

The environmental agenda has seeped into the mainstream. Labels like recycling, biodegradable, CFC-free and eco-friendly have become valuable marketing tools for companies which undoubtedly continue to cause much more environmental damage than they prevent. Many of the things we do or buy, and even aspects of our working lives, come with an element of environmental thinking attached. And where there's no quarrel with anybody else, most of us are all for it.

I've been building otter-hides down at Kylerhea on Skye. The Forestry is more conservation-oriented and such-like. That's took off in the last ten years. And it's very interesting, you get caught up in it yourself when ye're there day in and day out. Ye're generally workin' with a big squad, and they're all very interested in wildlife. They could tell ye the birds, some of them are very knowledgeable.

ALASDAIR MACKENZIE, *55, forester, Loch Carron*

Just as often, the changes in the ways we are thinking about the natural world breed the sort of misunderstandings which can lead to trouble. The hunt saboteur business became established as a fashionable hobby for students in the 1970s, while the huntsmen and women were acutely conscious of outsiders attacking their traditions.

I grew up here, and I must have gone out with the hunt first when I was about six. My father had a horse called Freddie which came second in the Grand National by a whisker; actually, he was second twice. And he was brought up on the farm, he would have been out with the hunt, and point-to-pointing. It's all part of country life, here. Though sometimes when I read articles about it, I think people just don't understand.

DOUGLAS TWEEDIE, *51, farmer, Middlethird Farm, Borders*

So the most encouraging aspect of a successful local environment-oriented partnership like Montrose Basin is the way it encompasses a range of people and attitudes. There's Ian Montgomerie, a man who has loved geese since childhood, is touched by the sight of them, and likes to shoot them. Well, actually, not just shoot them.

We perhaps roast two at a time in the Aga, an then have one for a roast with different sauces, an what's left will be made into a goose curry, or some o these different things. The flesh o the goose, if cooked properly, is actually very good, like the best steak.

IAN MONTGOMERIE

On the farm, geese have largely been seen as pests and enemies – and all the worse because modern farming practice has generally encouraged them. The EU policy of set-aside land means the birds can graze on stubble fields all winter, as well as on costly winter cereals like wheat and barley, and legal protection and conservation measures have seen geese numbers rising for fifty years.

But you get farmers at Montrose Basin, too.

Geese can do an awful lot of damage. If ye've got a full moon, they can come down on to a field of wheat in their thousands an bare it. But they can do good, too, clearin stubble, or eatin frozen potatoes and carrots in fields that have been lifted. An they're very easy to keep off. Ye just put out banger guns or scarecrows or whatever. Ye've got to strike a balance. I like havin them about the place. I've always looked upon them as bein a super bird. They can do the trip from Iceland to the northern coasts in one, an that's quite a flight. I went up to Iceland to see where they lived three years ago, an we went round the coast to see greylags an inland to where the pinkfeet live, a marvellous big volcanic area surrounded by glaciers – because that is their home. This is just a wintering-ground here. They've been around for thousands of years, I suppose. An they're just lovely.

RODDY MACKAY, 42, *farmer, Kirriemuir*

Out on the Edge

In Scotland we inhabit an edge – a country on the periphery of the Western industrialised world, the European continent, even on the periphery of the British Isles. And while something approaching 2500 of our 80,000 square kilometres are urban and fairly densely populated, the fact is that a great number of us are effectively on the periphery of Scotland itself.

Mail order, van deliveries and long journeys are the way of it out here – and an attitude which treats the self-importance of the distant centre with some scepticism. But there has been a nagging sense of marginalisation, too, along with the constant draining of youth and energy from the remote communities into the maw of the metropolis.

So it's all the more remarkable that the seclusion, sparse population and small-scale communities of Scotland's remote areas should have begun to attract more people than are leaving. The incomers bring ideas and impetus, and there's a new confidence out on the edges which draws strength from the increasing control of local land, community business initiatives, and new technology which circumvents the whole idea of a periphery.

It's true, the turnaround has caused tensions in places which have undoubtedly suffered from conservatism. But there's a resilience in our traditions; the rituals, celebrations and special occasions which we have honoured for generations are themselves bending to the new opportunities.

A Very Sheltered Life
THE REMOTE SETTLEMENTS

Scotland's barely populated, unusually beautiful wilderness brings visitors from all over the world. But the fact of it is that the same qualities which lend glamour to the landscape make life a constant practical challenge to those who actually live in the remote areas.

If we need new parts or repairs for the computers, we can't expect anyone to turn up in the next five minutes. But they'll turn up on the next ferry. Except in November, when the force eight or nine gales are blowing. And occasionally we have power cuts which can cause havoc; so we do have to be a bit more patient than people in mainland Scotland.

LYDIA HARDCASTLE, 37, *telecottage worker, Hoy*

There's just about seven houses in the whole of Papa Stour, and there's no streetlamps, and no noise at all. You can hear a tractor from the other side of the island. And from anywhere in the island, you can see the sea. But, once you've done anything on Papa Stour, if you do it over and over again you get bored. And if you're stuck in the house with your parents you tend to get on their nerves a bit.

SARA FOX, 13, *schoolgirl, Shetland*

Shopping here is a world away from the concrete malls of the city. The far-travelled essentials, from petrol to oranges, cost a fair bit more than in the Central Belt, and the choice is limited. Swapping and barter, and scribbled notices in the shop window or local paper, will often do for buying and selling goods. And the mail-order companies make handsome amounts of money in the Highlands and Islands (even if the letters columns of local newspapers regularly feature the anecdote of the islander whose order to a London firm has been answered by the likes of 'Unfortunately we are unable to conduct our business with areas outside the United Kingdom').

Lochinver being the biggest village on the west coast of

Sutherland, I carry deliveries like mattresses, small pieces of furniture from those catalogue places, and lots of supplies for the fishing boats; big, big boxes of oilskins and things like that. It's a bit of a problem, because once you get all these goods in, you cut the seats by half.

WALTER MACKENZIE, 39, *postbus driver, Lochinver*

Johnny the Bread, that's what they call me. I used to drive a bread van. Names stick to you up here. And even with the postbus, when I get to the end of my round in Talmine I've got about a hundred houses to deliver to – prescriptions, newspapers, milk, meat, everything. I know them all. And dogs give a problem sometimes; I've been bitten twice. But I know the ones that's a problem.

JOHN MACKAY, 61, *postbus driver, Talmine*

Ye get to know all the van drivers well, helping to dig them out o ditches or whatever.

GEORGE HOLDEN, 60, *farmer, Braelangwell Farm, near Ardgay*

The Scottish banks run their own mobile branches (the first ran on the island of Lewis in 1946) and the bread or fish vans delivering fresh food in outlying areas are generally small going concerns. But the costs of subsidising services like the postbus or the district nurse are substantial. And what price knowledge, out here? It costs hundreds of thousands of pounds each year to fund a dozen mobile library vans which tour the Highlands with some 3000 books each.

It's not the sinecure I expected after I retired from the RAF. There's an awful lot more to it than meets the eye. I know exactly what every reader in my van is interested in, whether it be Catherine Cookson – the most popular author, and the bane of my life – or whatever. I make individual calls at farms and crofts. And as I go round, I'm invited in for a coffee, and you get a ceilidh as they call it in this part of the country. And you become very intimate with them, you really get to know their family and all their problems. I go to old folks' homes, and schools – there's one school I visit outside Ardgay, and the children there are absolutely delightful. They are a charm, they really are. Except I've got one little blighter who's always looking for books on sex, a ten year-old. But I pre-empt him and take all the books off the shelves before he comes. You've got to have your wits about you. And when I come down to a seaboard village it really is hell, because there are so many customers. I can do 500 books in six or seven hours. And it's easy dispensing them, but putting them away ... And I have one fellow, an elderly chap – it's ten o'clock in the morning, and he's plastered out of his mind each time I arrive, away with the fairies, and God knows where he gets the drink from. Well. But my favourite days are the ones going up towards the Dornoch Firth. The countryside is lovely – single-track roads, crofts, farms, sheep on the road, that sort of thing. I've been stuck in the snow, had to borrow a spade from a local farmer or get help to push me out of a ditch, or a flat tyre stuck away up a glen. All the books come tumbling down, and one is left with 500 to put back, in alphabetical order.

GEORGE RAE, *59, mobile library driver, Sandwick*

George comes on a Thursday, about the middle of the day, and it's definitely a highlight of the week. No time is convenient for a farmer, but we make it convenient; it's something to look forward to. He stops for about half an hour, and has a cup of coffee, and we have a good crack. He's an interesting character in himself. And he's like the old-time postman in a way, he passes on the local news to us; and it's usually the hot news of the day, if anything's happened.

GEORGE HOLDEN

The alternative to waiting for the vans, if you're fit and have transport, is the long haul to the shops of the big city. Islanders from the Hebrides, Orkney and Shetland travel ferry and car journeys of many hours to reach the chain stores of Inverness. (And this may be 'the capital of the Highlands', but we're talking about a town which is much smaller than, say, Dunfermline or East Kilbride.) But the pattern is the same at every regional centre.

I think there's a Gateway supermarket in Invergordon. But a lot of our customers come from the outlying districts – the Black Isle, and down from Ullapool and Gairloch, and from the north. They make fortnightly or monthly trips, they say that makes it worthwhile for them.

KATHLEEN CAMPBELL, *50, supermarket check-out operator, Dingwall*

It's not just the shops which draw people in from the edges, either. In island towns like Portree, Kirkwall and Stornoway, and Highland centres like Fort William and Golspie, a troop of children from the remote areas arrive by ferry, taxi, bus and sometimes even plane to go to school. It can be the biggest uprooting in a young life, too, this journey from a far-flung settlement to secondary education.

It's quite a jump moving from the primary school. Shetland was completely the big city. In Fair Isle ye live a very sheltered life – even in Shetland ye live a very sheltered life compared to somebody living in Britain – and if I'd stayed there I wouldn't have been able to cope with anything more than Shetland. It would have been just too much culture shock.

INNESS THOMSON, *18, school-leaver, Lerwick*

I came over when I was eleven, and I was fairly homesick at first. I didn't find it too easy fitting in with the amount of people in each class, and changing classrooms. There were only six or seven children at the primary school in Foula, just one classroom and the same people all day. It's very different here, and I don't especially like Lerwick. I would say the people are quite different, because it's a completely different environment. But it is pretty interesting to meet people from the other islands.

MAGNUS GEAR, *14, schoolboy, Lerwick*

Villages throughout rural Scotland centre on primary schools which often have one teacher, one classroom and a handful of pupils. But there simply isn't secondary school provision on this scale. So, every year, children from the outlying areas have to board at local authority hostels attached to secondary schools many hours' travel from their families.

Only a few decades ago, schoolboys from the islands could find themselves staying with working men in town digs while they studied. Today, the accommodation is institutionalised in purpose-built complexes staffed by managers and 'house parents', with study bedrooms for older children. Typically, Anderson High School in the Shetland capital of Lerwick is a part-time home to more than 200 of its 900 pupils.

Usually it's two weeks at a time in the hostel, but it can be three or four weeks in the winter-time. The crossing takes about fifteen minutes in a nine-seater plane, but it depends a lot on the wind. If there's a north-westerly and more than fifteen knots you can't go. So ye don't really make specific plans for what ye're going to do. But I phone home most nights. Last night they were saying my cousin had bought a new fishing boat, and they'd been working with the sheep. I was telling them the kind of things I've been doing at school. And I'd seen a boat I thought my dad might be interested in. If I was there, I'd be helping out with mum and dad on the croft, or helping my dad with his lobster boat in the summer.

MAGNUS GEAR

You do get pretty homesick, and I miss my two horses on the island. But I didn't know if I'd make friends here, and it turned out okay.

SARA FOX

For youngsters who want to make their lives close to home when school finishes, it's far from certain they'll walk into a wage-earning role in the country. The forestry and farm work and fishing has dwindled, and the returns from crofting are small. But the tradition and the instinct more often than not is to close ranks and keep the available work in the family.

I'd been driving artics for a haulage company, taking fish from Lochinver to Aberdeen overnight, and at the weekends off to France and various places, before I started this job two years ago. My father drove this route for twenty years before the Post Office took it over.

WALTER MACKENZIE

I was born in Lochinver, and worked in the family business for about thirty years, a general merchant's. I didn't like it. It's not a good thing, working with your relatives. But I hadn't much option. There was no other work, like.

JOHN MACKAY

My parents had a guest-house, and my grandmother's family ran a coaching inn for the last change of horses for the hill before you come into Oban – so it's dyed-in-the-wool. And my three sons are being brought up in the business, like I was. They earn pocket money, and they meet so many interesting and different people from all over the world, and they learn to cook, and clean, and make beds, which is good. My oldest son is seventeen, and he can do a five-course meal for the guests.

MONIKA SMYTH, 43, *proprietor, Ardblair Guest House,*
Oban

If it wasn't for the distillery, probably there wouldn't be a village of Carbost, or it would be half what it is. My grandfather worked here. And it's a good job to have on Skye, because jobs are quite scarce.

KENNY BAIN, 38, *process operator, Talisker distillery,*
Carbost

Whisky is one business which looks likely to guarantee a measure of local employment far into the future. In the 500 years since James IV gave a Tayside monk the first licence for whisky production, the industry has flourished. Not only is it our most famous global export, but it's up there with computers as our most lucrative, worth about £2 billion to the annual balance of payments. But, (ironically, just like computers) it's far from a labour-intensive business.

Twenty or thirty years ago they used to mash the malted barley by hand, and there were forty people working here. But the management have whittled it away down with new processes and systems.

KENNY BAIN

Still, the distillery is a vital local employer in more than a hundred rural communities. Life in the Skye village of Carbost has been dominated by it for more than 160 years. On the shore of Loch Harport, sixteen staff use barley, yeast, and water to produce 1.5 million litres of Talisker whisky a year, bringing millions of pounds in tax to the Treasury, and income to Talisker's owners Diageo, the multinational corporation which controls forty percent of Scotland's entire whisky output.

It's a proud workforce in whisky, where a lot o people maybe their fathers have worked in it, an they're interested in the job an interested in the people. A really sort of traditional industry. The guys I work with are all locals, all crofters, all people who've been here for years and years. And west coasters are definitely different. They're more relaxed. They get through the work the same. But there's no rush.

ANDY MacDONALD, 31, *production manager, Talisker distillery, Carbost*

With the traditions of whisky-making in mind, it's worth remembering, too, that even officialdom – that dismal world of red tape and paperwork and legal technicalities – acquires a different perspective far from the cities.

For three years from '73 I was goin to glorious parts of Perthshire educatin farmers about VAT – oh, I could tell ye some stories. Most of the farmers had never really had anythin to do with the tax man, an they were rather nervous about it. But I used to go out and explain it to them, an they were most responsive once they saw the VAT man had a human face. And VAT has now been vilified, but at that time the people were absolutely wonderful to us. From Rannoch station to Amulree to Loch Tay, that was my area. And it was the most wonderful time of my life.

JOHN FOTHERINGHAM, 47, *Customs and Excise officer, Grangemouth*

Small business initiatives have been a feature of Highland life for many hundreds of years. In the past, the poaching of a deer from the hillside or a salmon from the burn has been a tradition in which, country folk might say, surpluses are levelled, hungry mouths fed, and the laird enabled to make the discreetest of gifts to his neighbours. The running of a small still, similarly, was invariably seen as something whose discreet simplicity never necessitated troubling hard-pressed officials who almost certainly had enough paperwork to deal with in any case. There are even occasional whispers that these traditions linger on.

SHADOW OF EXCISEMAN FALLS
OVER MOONSHINE MEMORIES
The shadow of the exciseman, for centuries the arch-foe of Highland moonshiners, is falling over plans for

a new museum on the Isle of Skye dedicated to the history of illicit distilling.

For despite assuring islanders of complete confidentiality, staff at Praban Na Linne, a small whisky producer, found it impossible to persuade anyone to donate the aluminium coils and vats that make up a traditional but illegal home still.

'People still fear attracting the attention of customs and the police,' said Murdo Campbell, one of five staff who work at Praban Na Linne. Sales administrator Fiona McGregor agreed: 'Everybody knows people in this part of the world who continue with the old ways, making their own home-made alcohol, but unfortunately it's not the sort of thing they want publicised.'

Scotland On Sunday, 26 January, 1997

A bit of this, a bit of that, mixing and matching is often the way of it when it comes to working out on the edge. Remote industries like Harris tweed and Shetland knitwear have rallied a little after suffering badly from foreign imitation and competition, and there is still work for hundreds of people in their own homes. At the same time, the growth of the luxury food market has helped small businesses like smokehouses. The crofting tradition fosters this sort of diversity, and the development of farming for salmon, trout, shellfish and lobster has provided another avenue for part-time work (even if, typically, more and more of the fish farms are owned from outside).

Most o them here are crofters. And I've got a croft, but I'm doing something a little bit different. I've got an oyster farm on the shore. I buy the oysters from Cumbria, let them grow for two or three years, and then pick out the big ones and sell them to restaurants on the island.

KENNY BAIN

To me, the telecottage can do anythin as good as the publishin in Glasgow or Edinburgh, an it's a hands-on thing. People work part-time a lot here, there's not that many full-time jobs, and if they can spend a few hours with the computers and then the rest of the day on the hills with the sheep – that's the way they like it.

STEWART SOMERVILLE, *30, swimming pool supervisor, Hoy*

My father works on the ferry-boat, and he's a crofter. Everybody on Fair Isle just has a whole collection of jobs. If something needs done, they do it.

INNESS THOMSON

If there's one single thing which imposes a pattern on this rural informality, it's 'the season'. Economic necessity in many settlements means life is structured around the arrival of the tourists. Many of the hospitality jobs start then, and the population swells not only with the visitors, but the seasonal workers who'll help to cater for them. Craft shops, tearooms, hotels and guest-houses, cruise boats, historic castles, caravan parks, information centres and many other little businesses emerge from hibernation around Easter, and brace themselves for the deluge.

It's when the tourists depart, though, that the real community business of the villages gets going. Many rural settlements have developed two identities as they get used to playing the part of summer hosts, and everybody looks forward to the day when the polite smiles can relax, and the social catching-up and the getting-together can begin again.

Arran Drama Festival is in late February, in Lamlash Community Hall. Ye couldnae have it durin the season because a lot o the people in it would be too busy. Mind you, it's amazin how quick the winter goes. Most of us go on holiday in October, an then before ye know it it's Ne'er day, and then wallop the season's there again.

JIM LEES, 47, *proprietor, Corrie Crafts and Antiques, Isle of Arran*

The depopulation of much of Scotland's periphery is a complex process whose strongest roots are in the Clearances and changes in the agricultural economy. The centralised, hi-tech, automated agri-industry has so outstripped the edges today that the farmers and crofters largely have their milk and bread shipped out.

The long, costly journeys to get to and from the isolated islands are seen as a particular handicap to the settlements, too, and gradually more bridges and causeways are reaching out to them. (The people of Vatersay were obliged to swim their cattle across the sound to Barra before a £4 million causeway was opened in 1990.) But on the island of Stroma, where my own great-grandfather was the grieve in the 1860s, the building of a fine new harbour without any decent regular ferry service just seemed to speed the island's desertion a century later.

Often carrying traffic to or from Glasgow airport, the small plane has become an important link to the outer isles, adapted to unorthodox facilities like the famous cockleshell beach runway at Traigh Mhor on Barra, (where the daily flight from Glasgow is timed to coincide with low tide) or the two-minute crossing from Westray to Papa Westray across Papa Sound (supposedly the shortest scheduled air flight in the world).

> I was with Loganair as a captain for a year, which was lovely, flying around the Western Isles. But a single-pilot operation in bad weather can be awfully demanding.
> CAPTAIN ANGUS MacDONALD, 52, *flying instructor, British Aerospace Flying College, Prestwick*

The remote air routes, like the ferries, remain vulnerable to much more dangerous forces than the weather. The political and commercial bartering over subsidies and profits is never-ending. In October 1996 the majority of the lifeline plane services to the Highlands and Islands were bought out by a company based in the Isle of Man, whose management shortly pledged that they would not maintain the routes if they couldn't make them profitable by the year 2000.

Life in the remote parts has only been sheltered through its isolation, which is really no shelter at all. And if you're young, and growing up in the wild places, there's still a strong impulse to get into the swim, to 'make something of yourself'. To come in from the edge.

> I've just done my last day of school. I will definitely miss it here – it's like a fine place to be – but I'd like to see what the rest of the world has to offer. It's just different aims in life. Some folk would be quite happy to bide in Shetland all their lives; the ones that leave school in fourth year or maybe fifth year, they're the ones that stay on. But most of the others have plans for going sooth.
> INNESS THOMSON

A Better Chance
NEW ENERGIES

A 1993 survey found that ninety-three percent of children in the Western Isles with three Highers or more were leaving the area when they finished at school. And so it goes on, the drain of Scotland's young people from the country to the towns (and from the towns to England, or abroad).

But in the last thirty years, for the first time in centuries, there has been a change in the trends. Against the momentum of a troubled history, there are now more people moving into rural Scotland than there are leaving it.

> I was born in Caithness, but I've lived most of my life in the North of England. I had a mother with itchy feet. I always knew I was going to go back north, though. I used to joke with the kids. I used to say, Outer Hebrides, here I come.
>
> JO MACKAY, 50, *postbus driver, Durness*

Often the incomers are returning to their childhood home. Even more frequently they are southerners, drawn by new work opportunities, property prices, or simply by the escape from urban problems. The population of cities like Glasgow and Dundee is measurably shrinking, while the numbers are rising every year in the Highlands, Orkney and Shetland, Grampian, the Borders, Dumfries and Galloway.

Many of the remote places have come to depend on this immigration. On the island of Coll, ninety percent of the population are incomers.

> I was born here, and I went off the island to school and then agricultural college, and then I worked in Africa for twenty-nine years. But I used to come back every year; my father had a post office and a shop at various times, selling reapers and Tilly lanterns and all that kind of thing, and he worked with crofters on the east end of the island, and bought their fish and sent it to the Continent, and made a

57

market. So I came back frequently; I even had a goat here, and I used to do some lobster fishing when I could. And it has changed. When I was a young boy we had rabbits, and fish were more plentiful, and we had dairy farms and haymaking, and we used to go and help bring in the peats, and pick the potatoes. There was more of a – not just a spirit, but a need for co-operation, and ye don't have that now. Now the RSPB have a big bit of the island, two and a half thousand acres, and the farms are bigger and fewer. But in 1984 we came back, knocked down the old house and built a new one, and we've been running it as a guest-house. Though there's probably only about fifteen or sixteen of us Collachs now, out of a hundred and fifty.

ROBERT STURGEON, 72, *retired United Nations officer, Coll*

Whatever their reason for coming, it's clear that very many of the new rural Scots have come for good.

I moved from Dundee in 1977, to work at Dounreay. An I don't see me runnin down to the seethin metropolises now. Weatherwise it's a bit wild here, ye know. But it's a nice place to bring your kids up. Ye can sleep secure in your bed an walk the streets in safety. An the Highland mañana mentality – there's nothin as urgent as tomorrow sort-o-thing. The only thing I don't like is the weather, particularly this year – winter never really stopped this year.

FRANK CHARLTON, 46, *electronics engineer, Thurso*

My mother was from Skye, and I came up from Glasgow for a fortnight's holiday and met my husband after about two days at the Sligachan; at one point about twenty years ago it was known as the marriage bureau, because it was the only pub in the area.

CATHY MacLEOD, 41, *tour guide, Talisker distillery,*
Carbost

I'm from Wiltshire, but I'd hate to leave Aviemore now. Where else can I walk down the streets quite safely in the middle of the night? I can go climbing or skiing, or go to a night-club if I want to or to the theatre in Inverness. I think it's a wonderful place to live.

SARAH JULIAN, 30, *station booking clerk, Aviemore*

The escape to a wholesome life in the country was a sunny fantasy for the generation who grew up in the sixties and seventies with little enthusiasm for the pollution, crime and bustle of the city. The countryside wasn't just the place where farmers worked and people went for holidays anymore, but the setting for a new way of life which was called 'alternative' with a kind of rebellious pride. These were young people who had the freedom to follow alternatives their parents' generation could never have imagined, nurtured by quasi-hippy notions of craft-making economics and rural self-sufficiency.

And while the reality was never all that close to the dream, a very great number of the trail blazers stuck in on their faraway plot, learned their lessons, adapted, and made it work.

I'd been working in Leeds, making my own jewellery for five years. And eventually Trish and I decided, as trendy people do at that sort of age, that we wanted to opt out. We sold up in 1975 and bought a cow shed in Carradale, and converted the cow shed into a house, and converted the tractor shed into a workshop-come-shop. And here we are. We've renamed the shop the Carradale Gold Foundry, and I make dress rings for high street jewellers. And it has its ups and downs, but overall we increase every year.

MIKE HURST, 47, *jeweller, Carradale*

We were in Edinburgh, an we thought we'd like it a bit further out. An when lighthouses started comin up for sale, the yuppies were sellin their flats in London an snappin them up, an we thought we'd sort o missed the boat. My wife's got family in Orkney, an we didn't think we had an earthly chance o gettin this one. But we did. We moved in one stormy day in February two years ago with a child, a kitten, two dogs an six puppies. There's three houses, the principal keeper's house and two cottages. We thought we'd do self-caterin, an we're hopin tae start up a cafe in the next couple o years. We've also done some candle-makin. An we're hopin tae go ahead with a sort o island-hoppin package-tours thing for tourists, with Hoy as the sort o hub. Well, I was a Portobello boy, but I always wanted tae be in the country. And I made it in the end.

STEWART SOMERVILLE, 30, *swimming pool supervisor,*
Hoy

Knightswood's fairly close to Clydebank as the bomb drops, it got a bit of a poundin, and my parents were evacuated to Arran durin the war. My sister was born here – she's the minister's wife – an I grew up with the island. An after our first child was born, my wife – we met here on holiday, like lots o people – my wife an I decided we were not goin to live in the city. There's nothin wrong with raisin kids in Glasgow, but I felt they would get a better upbringin. A better chance in life. A lot o people moved onto the island at that time in the early '70s, a lot of escapees from the urban thing . . . There was quite a migration onto the island, a lot o them set up crafts businesses.

JIM LEES, 47, *proprietor, Corrie Crafts and Antiques,*
Isle of Arran

Plenty followed in the wake of the pioneers, especially with outrageous house prices in the south making new economic sense of country life. The yuppies hit the trail, coasting their four-wheel-drive vehicles up to the gates of buildings which were about to find themselves turning into largely empty holiday homes.

And there's no point in sidestepping what happened then. It's been a time of some tension in the village. With real pressure on the working traditions which bound local people together for generations, they've also had to adjust in short order to the social and economic changes which have turned up on their doorsteps with a bunch of strangers.

And, it has to be said, often older strangers. One of the overt effects of the pull of a distant centre is a kind of marginalisation by age. In 1995, 48,000 Scots moved south across the border, and 44,000 people came the other way. And looking at the age profiles, you can't help concluding that what the centre (London, essentially) does, is take in young people, and export older ones.

I was an administrator in the Air Force, working in British embassies in Vienna, Santiago, Chile . . . And when it came to the point of retirement we thought – well, we're not going to find employment, and we'll take ourselves off into the country somewhere where it would be a wee bit easier to live off my pension.

GEORGE RAE, 59, *mobile library driver, Sandwick*

Carradale was a big fishing port, but like all fishing villages, things have gone slightly awry. And employment is a problem. A lot of people move to Campbelltown, and a lot of people – like myself – move here to retire.

GEOFFREY PAGE, 63, retired teacher, Kintyre

Peter and I are both on the village hall committee. We have dances, and whists October to March, a summer fête for the kids, and bonfire night. Bowlers use the hall, and the playgroup, and the flower show committee. But quite a lot of people have come into the area from south of the border, and they don't really want to be involved in things. There's a lot of retired people, and it's very difficult to get people to come and support a dance.

LINDA DOUGLAS, 28, farmer's wife, Ruletownhead

A lack of regulation has allowed well-heeled outsiders to overheat local property prices so that young people very often simply can't afford to stay in their place of birth. And there are other shades to this tricky picture, too. Many of the newcomers are lowlanders. Many are from England. In 1991, more than 350,000 people living in Scotland were English-born. And like many of the rest of us, the Sassenachs quite fancy country life themselves.

But keeping a perfectly straight face, I have to say it's possible that some of the southerners who move into rural Scottish communities may not be as sensitive to the delicate aspects of their situation as they could be. And on the other side it's maybe forgivable to suggest that, ruled by thrawn traditions over a very long time, their destinations are sometimes not the most cosmopolitan of places, either.

It can be very cliquey. From one village to another, nobody really knows each other. They have a tendency to stick to themselves.

JO MACKAY

Some o the articles in the *Carradale Antler* have perhaps been a little more contentious than they could be; the new jetty at Torrisdale stirred up a number of factions, and some of the articles got a bit strong. I'm certainly not against home truths. But in a small village, ye've got to be circumspect.

STUART IRVINE, 55, retired consultant, Carradale

Wickers still think we're Caithnessians, real Caithness people, whereas Thurso is the kind of atomic town. Thurso people are the influx from Glasgow or wherever that came up to Dounreay, and ye can tell the Thurso accent is all changed – it's a more polite sort o way, where we speak maybe a wee bit quicker.

PAT MILLER, *40, chargehand, Dounreay*

A sense of humour and a little perspective can go a long way; but comfortable extroversion and wary insularity were never going to be lovers at first sight. In a shrill echo of colonial-style abuses of the past, the locals know the incomers as 'white settlers'.

Yet the fact is, that with the old ways dying out, the rural population shrinking, and communities losing focus, the newcomers have reversed a trend which in many places looked terminal. Many of them bring a deliberate influx of new energy to the activities which give a place a reason for surviving.

I think the island has more than its fair share of creative folk, an that's a thing that's gone back years. The life-blood renews itself fairly frequently; people want to get out o the rat race, and they bring other talents with them, which is a good thing.

JOHN BRUCE, *46, teacher, Corrie, Isle of Arran*

I'm from Derbyshire originally, and I moved to Hoy eight years ago. I used to come on holiday regularly, and I got to know the place and the folk, and met my husband here. I'd been working in central Manchester doing computer sales for ten years, and I happened to mention that I knew a little bit about computers. That's why I got swooped on when the telecottage was getting going here. That happens here sometimes.

LYDIA HARDCASTLE, *37, telecottage worker, Hoy*

Village people, they're a law to themselves, They're very kind, but very demanding at the same time. In a village environment, people don't like outsiders comin in that aren't goin to put somethin back into the community. I've been involved with the Brownies, an I was approached by someone sayin ye would have to join the drama club, an I said no I wouldn't. However I turned up one night, an I was on the chorus line o the pantomime. An I was hog-roped an tied before I knew it.

ALEX ALLAN, *33, hairdresser, Birnam*

Some rural settlements have acquired a vital degree of flexibility, like Oban or Orkney, where the impetus of new industries like tourism or oil swept away many habitual attitudes in a relatively short period of time. But there are others where the transition is slow and painful. And it's hard to face up to the fact that these places must change, if they're not going to end up like St Kilda or Stroma.

Like many West Highland villages, we have had for a very long time this constant problem of the locals saying the white settlers are the ones who do everything.

STUART IRVINE

Unfortunately, with my job driving the postbus, I stepped into a local's shoes. And the Scots can be very abrupt, bolshie really. But I can understand that. We're white settlers, you know! And it was quite difficult at first. But I'm not one to be deterred easily. And coming towards Christmas it was boxes of chocolates and packets of biscuits and drinks appearing in the postboxes, and slowly it began to change. And after being divorced for twenty-two years, I met up with a postman. And we got married last October.

JO MACKAY

A lot of people have come in to Coll from the South, and they've got themselves working, quite a number of them. But I do wish more Scottish people would come in. It's always a bit of a risk in these kind of situations, though, if ye've got a house on the mainland. The cost o living itself is probably about twenty-five percent dearer here.

ROBERT STURGEON

Even in Westminster, there's a superficial consensus that the remote areas should be subsidised to protect the life of their inhabitants. Which is only as it should be, because it's constant centralisation from the south which has turned rural Scotland into an economic dependency. From the Clearances through the decimation of the fishing fleet and the railways, it sometimes looks almost as if a wealthy, distant, powerful clique have conspired to deprive a far-flung minority of any chance they've had of self-sufficiency.

Yet in the 1990s, almost unbelievably, it's beginning to look as if the fight for rural Scotland might be beginning to take the very big step beyond negotiating the terms of dependency, and into the world of self-determination.

The past few years have seen the healthiest outbreaks of confidence in living memory. The building of a bridge to Skye (and more precisely the banning of ferry competition in October 1995 and the imposition of mandatory tolls said to be the highest in Europe) produced an impressive community campaign of resistance. Intensive and clever lobbying in the late 1980s won millions of pounds for Gaelic broadcasting from the government at a time when it seemed Westminster was more likely to fund expeditions to Mars.

Assynt, Laggan and Eigg have shown what can happen when the periphery sets its sights on control of its own destiny. Other stepping-stones towards local empowerment include the beginnings of a new wave of mini-hydro projects which could see communities running their own generating schemes and selling electricity to the National Grid. There's something in the air.

> We get lots of letters from people who have ideas, whether it be harvesting water lilies, or all sorts of things. But it's not really for us to have all these visionary ideas; I think it should be for people on the ground, and we should be there to empower and enable them, and get grants and help. And I think the most important role we have is to be a sort of role model for other communities. The Assynt crofters have got such a high profile here, because we were the first, that I feel we should be seen to succeed.
>
> AILEEN KINNAIRD, 47, *teacher, Lochinver*

Assynt today pursues a community-based economy with the planting of forestry for future generations, income from angling permits and sporting rights, the beginnings of a careful tourism development based on taking outsiders temporarily into the community and showing them the evolution of crofting, plans for new, affordable housing for young people and even an international EU-funded research programme into the use of computers in land management.

And in this new, brighter light, the crofting system itself, involving a range of work on a few acres, begins to look like an attractive model for social units which could repopulate the desolate areas with a lifestyle which is fundamentally environment-friendly. Much of this is a great experiment, and much of it may not come off. But even in the most traditional, insular community, it can't be so difficult now to see the advantage of standing up and taking hold of change.

Basically Carradale is a fishing village with holiday interests, and a lot of people commute into Campbelltown. But there are changing patterns. Fishing has its problems, although they seem to be hanging on in there. But certainly tourism is taking an incredible downer around this neck of the woods. And basically the village is disappearing into a Catch-22. Well, I went in with both feet, and we had quite a successful meeting in the village hall where we set up a thing called the Carradale Propulsion Company with a bunch of local people who felt something could be done. We decided we'd pick on a few projects to look into – a total refit of the village hall, and looking at the use of the old school, looking at the harbour for yachting facilities, and trying to get a bit more oomph into tourism. And one of the things we wanted to do was get a form of communication into the village, like a monthly newspaper. People are very insular, they tend not to be get-up-and-goers, and I wanted them at least to know that things were happening around them.

MIKE HURST

New technology meant that the baby boomers needed little more than a typewriter, a photocopier and a single enthusiast to produce a new generation of community newspapers which could be a focal point and a forum for local issues, a cheap shop window for local advertisers, a record for posterity, and a bulletin board for the social, sports, and church events which bring people together.

We try to meet as many people's interests and needs as we can. The headmistress writes about the school Gaelic choir and there's the Brownies and the minister writes. There's a guy in the village just finished doing the Munros, so he's going to do a gentle column about that, which is excellent. And an old lady who used to live up the glen does these delightful articles of reminiscences. I failed my O-level English substantially the first time, but I do a leader occasionally. The last one was that there wasn't enough progress with the visitors' centre here. The typefaces are all different, and the photocopying's not brilliant, and you've got to sit and fold eight or ten pages an issue. It can be a total thankless pain in the bum; last night the photocopier broke down so this issue is late. But it cleans its face, and leaves a little bit over for the village hall refit fund. And it's no mega job putting out a newspaper, is it? In the school they read articles from the *Antler* on to tape for blind people in the village. Well, if everyone's nice to me it'll go on forever.

MIKE HURST

There's much, much more to come. In Thurso, men and women sit at terminals solving problems for 70,000 British Telecom mobile phone customers. There is a man at a computer in Fort William, translating manuals for Mercedes Benz in Germany. Children at Port Charlotte Primary School on Islay get their art lessons through a videoconference line which connects them to a teacher 100 miles away. Staff in Forres process parking tickets direct from the hand-held computers carried by traffic wardens in three London boroughs. And so on.

Computer technology needn't just be another way of working for somebody else's big business, either. A range of community-based 'telecottages', often funded by grants from Enterprise organisations, local councils and phone companies, have shown how remote settlements can hook up to the global village in all sorts of ways. The telecottage on the Orkney island of Hoy (population 450) is self-financing under a local management committee which includes its biggest users, English-born professional partners Lydia Hardcastle and Jude Callister.

I was born in Liverpool. And my husband and I had done a lot of work in Orkney as archaeologists, and we came up here with the idea that we'd take any sort of job to enable us to live here. We did bed and breakfast, and archaeological tours of the islands, and then Nick started working for a local builder and I became involved here. And we don't make very much money, but we have a good time! When you live in a place like this you can't always be choosy about what sort of job you get, and I think I'm very lucky to have found something that I find interesting and rewarding.

JUDE CALLISTER, *32, telecottage worker, Hoy*

The way the Hoy telecottage operates echoes many of the characteristics of the healthy settlements on the edge – rich variety, a bit of sharing, informality and flexibility.

We operate an open door here, and it's no way a hi-tech place at all. I have my little boy here after school, and the dog usually sleeps under the table. And all the island use us for something. We do all the church documents for the minister, and training for local residents, and some artists use our scanning systems to enhance their work and tweak it about. We've just done an access guide for Orkney Disability Forum – a fairly hefty tome; and Peter Maxwell Davies, the composer, who stays six months in quite a remote part of the island, and does weird and wonderful things all over the world the rest of the time – he comes here to fax his manuscripts to London. There's a botanist using the computer-based technology to produce his own database of the flora of Hoy and Orkney. And millions of databases throughout the world can be accessed by people who need information on absolutely anything. At the moment we're working on a project for a charity in London called Farm Africa. It's obviously a bit less expensive to get somebody at the top of Scotland working for you than it is somebody in central London. So they sent disks of text, and we're publishing two booklets for workers in North Africa: Camel Production in Kenya, and Improved Camel Marketing. So we know all sorts of things about camels now. What you can do with a camel when it dies is incredible – eat the meat, and use the hide and the teeth, and even burn the camel dung, you know. It is a bit bizarre; I don't think a camel has ever been seen in Hoy.

LYDIA HARDCASTLE

The biggest computer networking plan yet to unfold is the idea of a University of the Highlands and Islands which will link teachers to thousands of students across an area larger than Belgium. With the right equipment a professor can give individual tuition down the line to a student many hours' travel away, or lecture a class.

There's a big hurdle to get over with computers, even for my age group, and certainly a lot of people on the island. There's a fear of technology which the kids growing up with computers now don't have. I think it is the way forward; but I think it's going to take a lot longer to work miracles than everybody thought.

JUDE CALLISTER

But some of these ideas will work. And the principle seems clear: computer technology, creating a medium where the idea of a periphery makes no sense at all, is another way of bringing power to the edges. There's even a danger here, that something which is such a leveller across any distance and geography will distract, in its glittery, hi-tech way, from the real issues of place and people and power.

But there's no doubting the stirrings of imagination and self-belief in rural Scotland. And even if the young still leave to see the world, it looks as if there might yet be more for them to come back to.

A Very, Very Big Day
RITES AND CELEBRATIONS

While there is conflict on the land – laird and tenant, developer and conservationist, native and incomer – it's not the whole story. They all meet in the shop, the pub, the church. And there are special occasions when most of them will have a part to play, whatever their differences. These times might have to do with work, or local history, church, family life, or sport, but beneath their superficial differences most big days are the same in the vital essentials. Their origins, and the ritualistic way they are celebrated, have deeper roots than we may suspect when we're in the thick of it.

Our notion of the past has a hold which distracts from the greedy present, and many of our pageants involve a theatrical reliving of ancient scenes. The Up-Helly-Aa festival in Lerwick on the last Tuesday of January climaxes in the burning of a longship in tribute to Shetland's Viking history. The Border towns have the Common Ridings, recreating the patrolling of the town boundaries in the reiving days, when men, women and children would steal over the English border and make off with cattle and sheep.

The island of Foula, twenty-seven miles into the Atlantic from the Shetland mainland, and the settlement of Blarmafoldach, in the hills above Fort William, are among the handful of places which still celebrate Old New Year's Eve on 12 January (the custom predates the abandonment of the Julian calendar in 1752.) The rest of us, like our great-great-grandfathers, stick with the new-fangled Hogmanay.

Often the big days which draw people together involve a sporting contest – the point-to-point, maybe, the fell race, ploughing competition, or the village warfare of a traditional 'ba' game', where hordes of 'uppies' and 'doonies' hurl themselves into a rule-free stramash with the alleged aim of carrying a ball to the far end of a town like Kirkwall.

Where I live, Glenisla is one of the oldest an smallest Highlan Games, an it's what it should be – just the Games, there, in the middle of the field. It's good to see a Games like that still goin on. Everybody gets involved. If they're no actually competin, they're helpin in the background. An it helps keep the community alive.

JOHN DAVIDSON, 22, *shepherd, Glenisla*

Ceres in Fife, where a games was first held by the fighters returning victorious from Bannockburn in 1314, has a claim to host the longest-running Highland Games. And games day remains a very real focal point for hundreds of rural settlements, taking shape in farm fields and village parks around traditions which are not only generations old, but – if it matters – a link to the sporting customs of the clansmen.

My father's done this, an my grandfather's done it, an I must hae been fourteen or fifteen when I started throwin a stone around in a field. I suppose the shots would originally be cannonballs, but a lot o the Games hae rounded stones they've picked up in the rivers over the years. An a caber is usually a hundred pounds in weight, an anythin up to eighteen or nineteen feet long. I've got two cabers at home, but round here if ye haven't got one ye just go into the wood an look for a decent tree.

JOHN DAVIDSON

I don't know whose crazy idea it was, but one Sunday night in the Square Inn twenty-three years ago, somebody said – there's a fête comin up wi a tug-o'-war. An we've just come on from there. We've got three farm managers, tractor mechanics, a glazier, a drayman, an I'm a postman. An new people just seem to appear; another team folds, an a boy might come along, an ye ask him to pull for his place, like. We'll go to approximately thirty games in a year, sometimes as far up the telegraph in Scotland as ye can go. An most of the time we travel in a couple of cars, which can be squashed; one o the bigger boys is twenty-one stone. It's mostly farm people in the team, an the big problem we have at this time of year is harvest. An I wouldn't want it to rain heavily, because that spoils the games – but I don't mind if it's a wee bitty damp, so I can get my best team.

DANNY MURISON, *postman, Burrelton tug-o-war team,*
Mcritch Farm, Alyth

In fact these competitive days give a fair picture of the collision of commerce and tradition. It was the enthusiasm of tartanry-smitten Victorian high society which first propelled the Highland Games into widespread popularity, and there is a profusion of games across Scotland from the last week of May until mid-September each year, with the attention, sponsorship money and tourist audience increasingly concentrated on the larger events. The trend is the same throughout rural Scotland, even for occasions like the sheepdog trials which test the shepherd's skills.

A lot of the Highlan Games now are gettin big, an there's sideshows an funfairs an that, an it doesn't have the same atmosphere.

JOHN DAVIDSON

The sheepdog trials has probably got into a more moneyed kind o game in the last ten or twelve years. It is changed. Ye've got a lot o hobbyists, they've seen it on the television. But I don't see many more young fellows comin into it, shepherds' sons, or whatever. The Americans come in an take an interest. An ye had some great laughs in the old days, but there's a lot o pressure on some o these great dog men nowadays. Everybody seems to be wantin to win, an it takes a bit o the pleasure away.

JIMMY VEITCH, 63, *shepherd, Drumcairn Farm, Edzell*

For part-time athletes from all parts of Scotland, though, the far-flung competition circuit is an essential alternative to the amateur athletics clubs of the towns, offering prize money, camaraderie, and local fame. And maybe the fervour of the competitors themselves is the best guarantee for the future of days like these. Few professional athletes, in their multi-million pound stadia, before the television cameras of the world, in perfect conditions and ready to pocket indecent fortunes, are striving any harder than this.

I was Scottish Games champion for middle-distance runnin in '89 an then in '91. Ye accumulate points for the races ye win on the circuit, an this year it's pretty tight between me an my pal Donnie Campbell from Elgin. It's down to whoever wins the maist in the next three weeks. People say 'oh, your times are not very good', an ye say 'well, you try runnin on these tracks!' Ye're runnin on grass wi sharp bends, an Blairgowrie's been pretty bumpy the last couple of years;

a lot of stones an that. Anyway, ye cover your petrol an things wi the prize money. Ye can get twenty pounds at some places, or if ye go down to the Borders, ye can maybe pick up £100 or somethin like that. There's a lot of bookies an that in the Borders, they do a lot of bettin. But ye dinnae mak money. I wouldnae miss the games noo though. It's like a holiday every weekend; the whole family comes, the wife an the mother-in-law an the father-in-law, an the three children – they run in the children's races. It's a grand day oot.

CRAIG BELL, 30, *railway trackman, Blairgowrie Highland Games*

There's something important at the bottom of most of the big days, whatever they are. Don't be misled by the spectacle of the bride-to-be on a Saturday night, draped in 'L' plates and led by a gaggle of girl-friends who're clattering their kitchen pots to collect wedding silver from good-humoured strangers. This is serious stuff. In Tain, on the Dornoch Firth, the couple to be married have to go through a refined list of discomforts known, with fearsome directness, as a 'doing'.

There's probably about a dozen doins a year, nowadays. I did my Auntie Liz when she got married, and I thought it was great. I was only about twelve, and she swore she would get me back. And she did. Basically what happens is ye get grabbed, usually it's like unawares, an they hold ye down, an they make up mixtures of like eggs and flour and syrup – Michele's brother had stuff from the butcher's, it was absolutely gross, the stink was unreal. An ye sit in the back of a truck or somethin – we were on a tractor an trailer – and ye get covered in all this crap, an ye sit there an go all round the town, an all these cars follow behind ye, hootin their horns, so it's almost like a parade, an everybody comes an looks at ye. People think, oh someone's gettin a doin, an they look out the windows an wave. An you wave back. I was absolutely freezin, it was December. An then, what they did to us was, they dropped us off in the High Street, so we had to walk home. And then ye have four showers. I actually enjoyed it; I actually think it's part o the wedding. Mind you, that's not what I was sayin when I was washin my hair for the fifth time.

KAREN DENOON, *farmer's wife, 29, Tain*

In the serious events of life, these rites of passage connect us to our people and the world. And in farming country, one of the biggest social occasions is the climax of the entire working year: market day.

> A very, very big day, no question it's that. A lot of plannin an a lot of heartache goes into it. From start to finish the whole operation takes maybe six to seven weeks. But it's a very good atmosphere at the sales; a lot of money changes hands, ye know. At one time they only had about two or three marquees, an three sale rings outside, an the numbers have jumped. But it's still the descendants of the same families, sellin. There's always a couple o shepherds' bars, an there's a lot o beer flowin – when they come in from the hills, they manage to shift some stuff!
>
> WILLIAM DOUGLAS, 59, *fencing contractor, Lilliesleaf*

> It does have a carnival atmosphere, with all the surrounding business. There'll be a lot of people attending the sales that are not doing any business whatsoever, but who're there because it's an annual gathering.
>
> JACK CLARK, 46, *auctioneer, St Boswells*

Amidst the meetings and greetings, the drink and the food and the playing children and the homespun stalls and the hard-selling advertising stands, the big agricultural sales condense into a few hours the pay-off for a year's graft and uncertainties across tens of thousands of acres. And for the hundreds of farmers and their families whose livelihood is about to be decided in a crowded field, these can be the most vexing uncertainties of all. Here as much as anywhere, it's the ritual that makes things bearable.

> We've been sellin here since 1963, and this year I've brought 100 pedigree Suffolk rams – the largest consignment at the sale. Shearlings, we call them; they're just over a year old, an they've been shorn just once. We get a big artic an bring them down the night before, an then they're penned in here overnight. They're all trimmed up before they go; ye dress them with shears just like a hairdresser, an put a number on them, an put a bit of bloom on them, like a bride on their weddin day.
>
> TOM STEWART, 59, *farmer, Sandyknowe Farm,*
> *near Kelso*

It has taken two years' planning for the man that has bred a shearling sheep to be sold at half-past ten this morning – and the whole thing can be decided in ten minutes. It's poignant. You're standing there, the judge of the roup, and you're conscious that your client's income is in your hands. He'll have slept these sheep and dreamt them, they'll have become part of his family; and when he goes home from the sale, tomorrow morning he'll start work on the sheep for next year, and the sheep for the year after that.

JACK CLARK

Ye want a good sale, for one thing, so ye can pay the rent an pay the wages. There's years ye're very pleased with what ye get, an years ye're displeased. But I think this one should be okay. We've been quite lucky with where we're balloted to sell – about a quarter past eleven. It'll have been goin for an hour by that time, so they'll be settled into the trade. Ye don't want to be first.

TOM STEWART

Near the biggest markets, like the ram sales in the Borders abbey town of Kelso, guest-houses are booked up months in advance by farmers from all over Britain and even Ireland. Kelso's second Friday in September has turned into the biggest event of its kind in the northern hemisphere, with buyers spending as much as £20,000 on a sire for their future flocks.

And here again, it's no surprise that the trend across the countryside is for fewer, bigger events. People can travel easily, and the fabric of country life has loosened, so that even in rural areas the big days are becoming centralised. This doesn't only apply to market or sports days, either; there may still be local dances in dusty village halls, but the big-scale knees-up is a growing phenomenon.

In the old days I used to go round the hunt balls, an it was always just a way of huntin people enjoyin themselves. But now we're findin that the ball is very much supported by people outside the huntin field. It has a big draw. They might come down to the Borders from East Lothian, an Edinburgh.

DOUGLAS TWEEDIE, 51, farmer, Middlethird Farm, near Gordon

This isn't to say that occasions like the Berwickshire Hunt Ball, which has become one of the January fixtures in the Scottish 'society' calendar, are entirely divorced from the local community. This big day's history is as long as that of the Berwickshire Hunt, which began meeting in the early 1700s, and it has recently been held at Manderston House, the stately home near Duns owned by Lord and Lady Palmer, of the Huntley and Palmer biscuit family.

> The Hunt Ball by tradition has been a full-blown affair and for some reason it has got this name as a very smart hunt. But it's not at all; it's very much a people's hunt. This year at the Ball we have Alistair Grant, the chairman of Safeways, and a fair number up from London, as well as a lot of the members of the Hunt, and really anyone interested in country pursuits. And the hairdresser from Duns.
>
> LADY CORNELIA PALMER, 40, *Manderston House, near Duns*

Some might say clues like the champagne reception and unlimited drink, seafood bar, full breakfast after midnight and Scottish reels in the ballroom, reveal the discreet perpetuation of the us-and-them class divide which has been a way of life in rural communities for centuries. But life in the 'big house' is rarely easy for those who inherit it today. Manderston House's 100 rooms are now run as a business, hosting hunting parties and corporate entertainment and even film crews. And if that means that some of the old traditions are exploited for their fiscal value, well its defenders might say that at least it is the traditions which benefit.

> The hunt employs huntsmen an professional staff to run the kennels, an ye've got vehicles; an with only thirty to forty subscribers, the finances are made up by runnin events, like the point-to-point an the ball. We start off by sendin out invitations wi the hunt crest on the front, an the ball is quite a fund-raiser now. The tickets are not cheap, an demand is good.
>
> DOUGLAS TWEEDIE

My father used to hunt, an my son hunts now, but I never have myself. I was feared o bein on a horse's back as much as anythin – unless it's an awful docile animal. But the Hunt

Ball is somethin we look forward to. We've come with the same group o people for several years, mostly local farmers, an nowadays we hire a minibus from Chirnside or Duns for breathalyser reasons. There's a wide range of people from all walks of life – wealthy farmers, the more ordinary farmers, lots of people come from Edinburgh, an I believe from London as well. We all have our other activities, but it's certainly one o the social highlights of the year round here. An it's support for the hunt as much as anythin; they've been very good with liftin our fallen beasts.

QUENTIN LINDSAY, 52, *farmer, Foulden Hill Farm, near Chirnside*

It is a big responsibility, and it is nerve-racking, because you worry about the damage. People do get a bit wild, and you have to watch one or two for the drink.

CORNELIA PALMER

Ah yes. There is that other important ingredient, along with the tradition and the community, which crops up in nearly everybody's tales of the big days. The drink.

It's hardly surprising that there's nearly as many Scots words for the bevvy as there are for getting blootered. It's one of our specialist subjects. The history of alcohol in Scotland is a long and colourful one, encompassing the legendary lost heather ale, the centuries of the Auld Alliance with France and its rivers of brandy and Bordeaux wine, and of course the multi-billion pound exporting whisky industry.

And let's be frank about it: most of us are kind of partial. You could almost say we're looking for an excuse. The ceilidh, the party, the dance, the birthday, the retiral or promotion, the leaving or the returning, the stag and hen nights, christenings, engagements, weddings and wakes, the team victory or defeat, the Saturday nights, the Friday nights, the nights in-between. On the island of Eigg, which has no pubs, the excuse comes daily with the ferry.

The *Shearwater* comes six days a week from Arisaig, and people do go down for a drink in the bar. Usually it comes in for half an hour, leaves and goes somewhere else, and then comes back for another half an hour. But occasionally it does sit in all afternoon, and lately that's tended to be Saturday

Michael Murphy (centre) with sons Lawrence (left) and Gerard, Motherwell.
(Paul Hackett/Scottish Media Newspapers)

Malcolm Mackay and Alasdair Mackenzie, Skye.
(Paul Hackett/Scottish Media Newspapers)

Joyce Cameron, Kathleen Campbell and Julie Montgomery, Dingwall.
(Scottish Media Newspapers)

James Marshall, Allan Corbett and Jamie Webster, Clydeside.
(Ian Hossack/Scottish Media Newspapers)

Tracy Mearns, Susan Grant and Gerard Hamill, Bellshill.
(Edward Jones/Scottish Media Newspapers)

Javed Akhtar (centre) with sons Asif (left) and Atif, Govan.
(Maurice McDonald/Scottish Media Newspapers)

Lesley Quigley, Marina Rea and Gillian Ferguson, beneath Glasgow.
(Angela Catlin/Scottish Media Newspapers)

Jim Buchanan, Donald Macrae and Nevis Hulme, Loch Maree.
(Ian Jolly)

afternoons – and some days it's mobbed. But it's a great wee
gathering-place. On a sunny afternoon you can sort of sit out
on the deck, and have a drink, and have a bit of a crack . . .

MAGGIE FYFFE, *48, secretary, Isle of Eigg Heritage
Trust, Eigg*

There again, some people can make a party anywhere, and no
excuses required.

A lot of the fiddlers an that come down from Shetland on the
boat – they'll be in the bar, an start up the fiddle music an
that, an it gets quite lively when it's busy. They get a wee bit
the worse for wear, but there's never any trouble or anythin
like that.

ALEXANDER COULL, *37, bosun*, St Sunniva

It's mostly unemployed an pensioners down here, an the
allotments seems tae be what they turn their time tae. Some
o the pensioners, they're there first thing in the mornin till
last thing at night. There's quite a few old Irish fellas, too,
an they'll tell ye a tale or two. An there's an old fella there,
he makes wine out o turnips; it'll blow your heid off, right
enough.

JOHN HADDOW, *47, high-rise caretaker, Budhill and
Springboig allotments, Glasgow*

However great the victory, though, however wild the dance; however many drinks are taken, there is one hard fact about the country's
big days which is second-nature to everyone. At day's end, the
routine of life is waiting. It always was.

We can't afford tae have too many jars; we've got tae be up
at seven o'clock tomorrow tae start strippin everythin down
again. Two or three weeks, it takes.

WILLIAM DOUGLAS

Tomorrow, it doesn't matter if I'm hungover or not; I've still
got my cattle to feed at half past seven. I'll probably feel like
death cooled-over, but it just depends on what time we get
home. Half past four? It's barely worth goin to bed . . .

QUENTIN LINDSAY

Children of the Revolution

History's a powerful thing in a small country. Look at this: across the Atlantic, a nation lapping up a cocaine-laced fizzy caramel health drink. Over here, a people who drink a rust-coloured beverage containing ammonium ferrum citrate and a whacking measure of proud mythology. It's hard to imagine any other Western nation so smitten by its industrial heritage that it would buy wholesale into a concept like 'Iron Brew'.

But then the cradle of the Enlightenment was also the engine-room of the Industrial Revolution, and towering heroes were born among the girders and rivets. It was the ironmasters and the steelmen, the railwaymen and bridge builders and engineers who made Glasgow the second city of the Empire, and made Scotland an equal partner in the forging of the industrialised world. The Forth Bridge, the flare of the furnace, the hurtle of the lift in the mine-shaft, the pumping of locomotive engines – the images are still powerful, played out to the constant hammer of metal on clanging metal.

Yet this was an adventure which distorted the shape of Scotland in a way which lingers even today. In the end its great achievements, like the railway network which opened up the country to its own people, were allowed to wither in the face of more pressing short-term profits,

And the pattern in which the farmers and fishermen took on the challenges of the natural world, built a life to support themselves, and now find the foundations of their communities pulled away by distant decisions, is echoed in the experience of the urban generations. The hundreds of thousands who flocked to the overcrowded Central Belt also lost out doubly, taking on a life of dangerous, poorly paid, miserable work, building the social underpinning to support it, and then finding the whole package wiped away as one by one the industries failed. Today we still suffer the legacy of unprecedented centralisation, still blighted by urban malnutrition, poverty, demoralisation and over-crowding.

Amazingly, post-war governments repeated the entire process of the Victorian industries in miniature with a series of disastrous set-piece industrial initiatives from which local communities are still reeling today. It's disturbing to conjecture what shape we might be in if the miraculous windfall of North Sea oil in the 1970s hadn't turned up to soften the economic and social horrors.

It Was a Style.
It Was a Way of Living.
MINERS

No doubt we like to sentimentalise, and to sidestep the grinding human cost of the Industrial Revolution. But it's hard to harbour any illusions even after a second glance. The economics of empire-building were based on the cruellest mathematics. And of the hundreds of thousands of lives which were counted cheap, very few lost as badly in the arithmetic as the men who went down the mines.

> Oh, coal is black an' coal is red,
> An' coal is rich beyond a treasure;
> It's black wi' work an' red wi' blood—
> Its richness noo in lives we measure.
>   from the song 'The Auchengeich Disaster', Tormaid

My wife would say – 'Shut the whole lot o the pits down; it's the best thing that ever happened.' An when I look back at some o the things that I've experienced, I think it's more because o nostalgia that I wouldn't agree. Her grandfather, uncle, an cousin were all killed in the pits. I started workin in the Barony in Ayrshire, where ma father worked from when he was eleven to when he was sixty-nine. He died of pneumoconiosis. Then the Barony became idle in '62, when the shafts melted away. Four men died, includin a man I was very friendly with. They were entombed. They are still there.
GEORGE MONTGOMERY, 69, *retired miner,*
49 Edmonstone Road, Danderhall

When it was wintertime, it was a case of dark o'clock to dark o'clock. It's a soul-destroying experience, and there were times when it was wet, you used to wear oilskins, and oh God, it was shocking sometimes. Three foot was the highest we had at Woolmet; two foot, depending on the seams. When that closed I was at Monktonhall for a couple of years and I got this chest trouble; they took an x-ray, and said if you don't get out of the pit you'll not be here in six months. It took me about a year to recover and get back to some kind of health. They'd told me I had bronchitis, and it was only five years ago I found out I have these big scars on my lungs, which they now reckon is certain to be pneumoconiosis or silicosis, from the dust in the coal, or the dust in the stone.

MAURICE TURNER, 74, *retired miner,*
45 Edmonstone Road, Danderhall

I started on the coal-face at the Woolmet in '52. But the roof came in on top of me in 1964 and trapped me, it took five o them to get me out. I had a burst lung and quite a lot of injuries. I was out for a year, an then I couldn't do face-work after that.

CHARLIE 'CHIC' TIERNEY, 72, *retired miner,*
116 Edmonstone Road, Danderhall

After the Barony shut I came to Danderhall, an became a safety inspector for the miners. In twenty-three years I investigated 156 fatal accidents in Scotland, an that was only half o them. There was a number took place when I was livin in Danderhall – people I knew well, and ye don't forget these things. People are pleased it's no at their door, an that's mixed with emotion because it's at somebody else's. Every minin family has connections wi accidents an people lost.

GEORGE MONTGOMERY

The industries which boomed on the back of dangerous and sometimes deadly conditions bred an unusual bond, and the sense of community grew strong in all the settlements which sprang up around the work. Even today, the comradeship remains fundamental. In old age, many ex-miners are still pursuing claims for the terrible toll the work took on their health. And mostly, the survivors stick together, often still living in miners' houses in colliery communities. You'll find them congregating at the old clubs like Danderhall Miners' Welfare near Dalkeith, by the old Woolmet pit.

It was a hard life, but there's a great camaraderie in the minin industry. Ye might no enjoy it at the time, but lookin back, ye realise what it was. I think a lot o miners, because o the segregation, where they lived in groups o houses like Newtongrange, a lot o miners think they're special. They lived together, worked together, an played together. They saw each other in the street, in the bath, at the coal-face, on the doorstep. It's no unnatural that a tremendous bond would develop.

GEORGE MONTGOMERY

It was a style. It was a way of living. You're a miner as you're sort of bred one, and it's a part of you. My foster-mother's brother worked in the pit known as Rob Roy, in South Yorkshire. It was a mining village, and every Friday they used to let me away from school to go and fetch his wages at the pit about a mile away. Then when I was fourteen I started at the pit bottom in Houghton Main colliery, getting hutches from one side of the colliery to the other by a sort of compressed engine on a rail. And I've always liked it. I must admit that when I came to Scotland, the Woolmet was a happy pit. There wasn't a day you couldn't roar with laughter. And I think that's what kept us going.

MAURICE TURNER

Pride is the single most surprising quality in the words of the working men who found their traditions slipping away. These were characters who made heroes of themselves, and camaraderie wasn't the only weapon they could draw on to fight adversity. The industrial communities bred a passion for self-improvement. From their own resources, their people became orators and politicians, artists, teachers and famous musicians.

The culture was good – the pipe bands, the silver bands, anglin clubs, golf clubs, bowlin clubs. They'd built it all up out o nothin. An these things are irreplaceable.

GEORGE MONTGOMERY

Like ma father, I started playin in colliery pipe bands in East Lothian when I was fifteen. Side-drum. There were so many pits, an they all had a band. There was virtually a band in every town until the pits were wiped out. An it was like a family, the Woolmet band. There was a very strong bonded friendship between the people that were in it.

WILLIAM GOODALL, 37, *university lecturer, Dalkeith*

Ye Tend Tae Be Just a Wee Bit Closer

SHIPBUILDERS

Great talents grew up among the cramped communities which weathered the giddy maelstrom of the booming Victorian industries. Three of football's greatest managers, Matt Busby, Bill Shankly and Jock Stein, all came from the coalfields. One of the greatest today, Alex Ferguson, started as an apprentice in the Govan shipyards. Even through the 1960s, the yards were populated by Clyde-built generations whose gifts went far beyond the welding or riveting tasks they were put to. Some are known today for other things, such as the comedians Chic Murray and Billy Connolly, the actor Russell Hunter, Hollywood screenwriter Alan Sharp or former Scottish Television boss Gus Macdonald.

And like the mining, the jute-spinning in Dundee, or the work at the vast Singer sewing-machine factory in Clydebank, shipbuilding was an epic business. At the peak of the industry on the Clyde, the men and boys who worked for poor wages and in harsh conditions were turning out half a million tonnes of shipping every year. Concentrated into a tiny riverbank pocket beside Glasgow was an industrial Cecil B. DeMille production, from the gargantuan vessels which loomed half-made at the end of the tenement streets to the tens of thousands of cloth-capped men who swarmed through the yard gates at the blow of a whistle.

Like the mining towns, too, the communities which had grown up shared disaster and consolation, a sense of common interest, of togetherness in adversity. And a special line in patter.

Clydebank took a real poundin durin the war, an there's a story . . . The bombers're thunderin overhead, an the buildins are shakin, an this family are runnin doon the stair tae get tae the Anderson shelter outside. An they've just reached the door when the old guy turns roon an starts goin back up again. Maw shouts efter him: 'Dad – what ye daein?' He shouts back as he disappears: 'I forgot ma false teeth.' She stares efter him a minute. 'What d'ye think they're daein, Dad – drappin pies?'

JIMMIE MacDONALD, 42, *architect, Glasgow*

There's so many jobs ye can be doin without. If ye're workin in the open air it's no so bad, but if ye're in a confined space it does get very warm. Sometimes ye can be squeezed intae a tank. An there has been jobs I've been home at night an dreadin goin in the next mornin. If ye're weldin overhead, the sparks an stuff fall on top o ye. Ye can get burnt quite a bit.

ALLAN CORBETT, 33, *welder, Govan*

The shipyard workers are a special breed, like the miners; if ye work in a hard industry, ye tend tae be just a wee bit closer.

JAMIE WEBSTER, 43, *welder, Govan*

I'm called Corky round here. It stems from I play football as a goalkeeper, cause when ye came intae work some people knew ye. Have ye ever tried tae get rid of a nickname? But I think most people in the yard have got a nickname o some sort. Jamie Webster's Spider, an James Marshall is Beetle, an there's a guy called The Pig, and Scattercash, for the obvious reasons. There was a guy in here, a foreman, was called Bertie Beetroot cause his face was purple a' the time.

ALLAN CORBETT

In the century after the *Comet* – the first commercial steamboat to sail on open water in Europe, launched on the Clyde in 1812 – Scotland's reputation for marine engineering was unequalled. And, as with all the Victorian industries, the way of it was that the great engineers and entrepreneurs caught the manufacturing tide, and the working man picked up the heavy tools.

But the decline of manufacturing industry in Scotland was pervasive and catastrophic. The twentieth century brought lively international competition and a new technical scene, and when suddenly the inheritors of the empire had fallen back in the race, they proved fatally slow to change. The tables were turning. It's entirely representative that the last jute mill in Dundee – the dregs of an industry that once employed 45,000 Dundonians around 'the richest square mile in the British Empire' – should these days be owned from Calcutta.

The badly managed shipyards had begun to falter even when the great transatlantic liners *Queen Mary* and *Queen Elizabeth* were built in the 1930s. And after the Second World War, government blunderings failed to halt the slide. The combination of nationalisation and gallus unions went a long way to countering the appalling working conditions; a very long way indeed.

I came in here in about 1970, efter ten year in a wee engineerin firm. That was ma first time in a yard, and I couldnae believe it. It was British Shipbuilders then, and it just seemed tae be people just walkin aboot, it seemed tae be money for nothin. People could do nothin a day, an naebody would say anythin aboot it.

JAMES MARSHALL, 47, *welder, Govan*

The unions used tae have a lot o power an influence. I'm no sayin the management were afraid o them. But they were wary.

JAMIE WEBSTER

I used tae think it was easy in here, until once, our work was slack an they transferred us over tae Yarrow's. I wore out a pair o' boots in six weeks wi just walkin aboot. They'd gie ye a two-hour job, an ye'd keep it for a week. It was Government money – a blank cheque every week.

JAMES MARSHALL

Managing directors will tell you that the power of the unions was one of the things which dragged down Scottish heavy industry, and certainly, from the mines to the steelworks, strikes were a feature of the decline. But poor labour relations were a beast which the well-heeled bosses had created themselves. And even when the future looked its bleakest, both the sense of community and the pride of the working man held fast.

In the last days, as was to happen elsewhere in Europe, the politicians underestimated the resources of a special breed of men who had grown up at the sharp end. When the Government abandoned the shipbuilding industry at its time of greatest crisis in the early 1970s, a remarkable thing happened. Hundreds of workers, fronted by Jimmy Reid and Jimmy Airlie, picked up their tools in the officially closed Upper Clyde Shipbuilders' yards, and carried on making ships. It was a national sensation.

I remember the time o the UCS work-in quite vividly. The Government was determined tae break the whole o the Clyde, an the workers took over the yard. It had never happened before, an it'll never happen again. The workers really did identify wi each other, an they motivated a lot o the guys tae dig in. They asked some o the apprentices tae go doon tae London for the big rally in Trafalgar Square, an I was lucky enough tae go. An the outstandin thing I remember is, the cheques started comin in. Ye really felt ye had the support o the whole o the country. No just the workin people, but everybody in Britain. Cheques comin from everywhere. It was unbelievable. Ye never forget aboot it.

JAMIE WEBSTER

But there was to be no long-term salvation. Like all the other children of the Industrial Revolution, the shipbuilders found their day had passed. Within little more than a decade the story was the same in the coal industry. And with virtually a whole way of living wiped away, there is still a sense of a fight lost; because under tremendous pressure from outside the working men did, together, try to resist the tide which was against them.

There's a feelin of – not despair through poverty, because most o the miners, they've got their pay-offs an their pensions – but there's a feelin o sadness. A feelin o helplessness. Because the industry went down so much, they'd nothin tae fight back with.

GEORGE MONTGOMERY, 69, *retired miner, Danderhall*

We got the yard saved. But there's been lots o crises since. The Government was determined tae offload shipbuildin, an they got their revenge. But that was twenty or thirty year ago. An the community here still identifies wi the shipyards.

JAMIE WEBSTER

Where less than fifty years before 100,000 men had been employed in thirty-seven yards by the biggest shipbuilding industry in the world, the old Fairfield yard in Govan became the last major merchant shipbuilding centre in Britain when the Norway-based multinational Kvaerner bought it in 1988. Today, the famous Clyde names – John Brown's, Denny's, Scott-Lithgow, Alexander Stephen – linger in legend. And, still, on some of the finest ships which sail the seas.

A Bit of Earache
THE RISE AND FALL OF THE RAILWAYS

There are, on average, sixty-six people to the square kilometre in
Scotland. The equivalent figure in England is 373.

When you've got so much place and so little populace, getting from
one place to another is quite an issue. And it's become a fairly troubled
issue, aggravated by our on-going history of centralisation. As the local
bank, bakery, post office and community hall close down, the villages
which used to make up the outskirts of our towns are becoming simply
suburbs; and the villages which were once rural centres are virtually
dependent on transport to distant towns. As we've seen in earlier pages,
long-distance vans are essential out here.

> I'm five miles up the road from Ardross, more or less sitting in
> the middle of a wood. It was once the kennelman's house for
> Ardross, and my husband's parents lived here. And I ran the
> sub-post office here for twenty years, after my husband had
> poor health. Until I was seventy. And at my age, ye no longer
> have your own transport. So I'm dependent on the post bus.
>
> ELSPETH THOM, 77, *retired sub-postmistress, Ardross*

Since the first post bus was introduced in East Lothian in 1968, the
Post Office has become an important player in rural public transport.
Nearly 150 post buses carry not far short of 100,000 passengers a
year in Scotland, as well as the mail, and other deliveries.

> I had a murderer on the bus once. Four or five years ago. He
> left all his clothes on the bus with a bag and said he'd be back to
> collect it, and I never saw him again. I didn't know who he was,
> but he'd murdered a woman in Talmine. When the police caught
> him, we were all set to go to the High Court in Edinburgh; but
> the man committed suicide. Another time I was taking ducks
> in a box up to Altnaharra, and they got out the box, and they
> were flying round the bus. I had a job sorting that one out.
>
> JOHN MACKAY, 61, *postbus driver, Talmine*

The year 1968 is the clue to what's going on here. Funded by fares revenue, charges for local goods deliveries, and government and local council subsidies, the post bus appeared in Scotland at just the time when the savage pruning of the railway network in Lord Beeching's name was taking effect. The disappearing trains meant that some affordable alternative way of allowing people to move around the country simply had to be found.

> This isn't a job for anyone who doesn't enjoy driving. One hundred and seventy miles from Durness to Lairg and back again every day, mostly on single-track roads. And there are some lunatics about when the foreigners get here; we do have some near misses. But I don't have time for boredom. The scenery goes with the weather, and the traffic's always different, and the people are always different. There's quite a few regular passengers; you might get some of the girls going to work in the hotels, and the dentist is in Lairg, and the driving school, and things like this. And they all yak to each other; it's a real hive of local gossip and information.
>
> JO MACKAY, 50, *postbus driver, Durness*

Only sixty or seventy years before, much of Scotland had been built around the tracks. The Victorian railways opened new frontiers for trade and tourism, and gave Scots a previously unimagined access to their own country, from the outposts to the industrial heartland. Spectacular engineering feats, tunnels and viaducts and bridges linked a network of more than 3500 miles of line through the most challenging terrain, and the railway itself was one of the great industries of the age. The giant russet frame of the Forth Bridge became a symbol of what was possible.

Suddenly people could live at a distance from their work, and suburbs grew up next to the cities. Round Scotland's edges, too, freight and other traffic turned into a booming business. At the goods yard, the station platform, the level crossing, on the journey into new places, trains became part of everybody's lives. The remote Sutherland fishing village of Helmsdale, on the north coast, had 100 railway employees as recently as 1956.

> I've always been around railways and railwaymen. The old Inverness-Aberdeen line intersected the fields on my father's

farm, and we used to curse like hell at the LNER steam engine drivers. They'd open the steam valve to scare the horses as they came past. But I still live quite close to the railway. And ye're always alert to hear the trains – it's an automatic thing, ye look at your watch to check it's on time. It's grained into ye.

GEORGE ALLAN, *59, station porter, Aviemore*

I joined the railway at sixteen as a signal-lamp boy in Keith. It was steam trains then, and ye had to walk away out to the distant signals an put a ladder up, an clean the lamps and put paraffin in. It wasnae so funny in the wintertime. Then I was taking the numbers of the goods vans to be marshalled in the yards. It was a busy station, a big junction. There was about 400 in the local sheds at that time. Aviemore was the same. It's only a village, an that was all there was.

WILLIE CRUIKSHANK, *51, station booking clerk, Aviemore*

But this century has not been happy for the railwaymen. In 1923 the 'big five' Scottish railway companies were forced to surrender their local independence to English companies in the south, and not long afterwards the bulk of Scottish railway engineering was drawn across the Border. Then post-war nationalisation cleared the way for the kind of commerce-oriented slash-and-burn which only makes sense if you've got your head buried in the plus and minus columns of an accounts book. Or a love letter from the motor industry lobby.

> . . . it's different today, for the railways dinna pay
> So they called in Doctor Beeching, oh.
> He came straight from ICI, in his pukka old school tie,
> You should just hear the nonsense he is preaching, oh.
> from 'Doctor Beeching', a parody of 'The Bonnie Lass of Fyvie', collected by David Mellors from a Mrs Kirk in Worksop

There's now not much more than 2000 miles of railway track in Scotland, and the cuts came in exactly the places where the train was most precious. Half of all the stations today are in the area around Glasgow.

At one time, when things was going great guns, ye did feel as though ye belonged to a big family in the railways. Ye

got to know faces for quite far around, guards and drivers
from Perth and Inverness, and ye'd get a very good working
knowledge of the country geographically. But things have
changed. There used to be a night-shift here for the mails and
papers for the Elgin area, and at Kingussie for Fort William.
But that's all away, they're putting everything on the road
now. And it's a bit rare to have staff in a station now. I used
to do relief cover at Carrbridge, until they unstaffed it, and
Newtonmore, and they unstaffed that two years later.

GEORGE ALLAN

While the railways withered, vast mountains of government money
were being redirected. By the 1960s, the modern age of transport
for the whole of Britain was there to be seen, emerging gleaming
from the assembly lines. The future was on four wheels, like Toad.[1]
Poop-poop!

On the road.

And it's a funny thing. Everybody used to love a train driver.
Remember waving from the bridge or the side of the track as he rattled
past on the rails? And yet, apart from their mothers, you won't find a
great number of people with a good word for the poor truckers.

People don't really like lorry drivers. Ye get quite a lot o hassle.
Sometimes ye have to sit a long time an wait if ye're unloadin
at a shop, or if ye're double-parked ye get a lot o hassle from
motorists an just everybody, really. An ye get quite a lot o hassle
from the police, an the commissioners from the Department of
Transport, they can pop up anywhere and stop ye for roadside
checks an that. But I just plod away an get on with it.

NEIL CRAIG, *30, lorry driver, Aberdeen*

It makes you wonder why we've been putting train drivers out of
business, and replacing them with unimaginable fleets of lorries.
But the strange thing is, there's still a lifestyle, a way of seeing
yourself – a romance, even, about life on the road. At least, to lorry
drivers.

I've always wanted to be a lorry driver. I suppose glamour
would be a part of it – just up an down the road, an your
own boss, kind-o-thing. An I got ma test for my twenty-first
birthday from my mum and dad – I was workin on the farm

at the time – an I got a job drivin tippies, an then I got the job wi Sandy. An it's been grand.

NEIL CRAIG

Ma father was a lorry driver, so I've always been that way inclined. I thought it was great when I was younger, like. He drove for a local firm in Stonehaven, an I used tae go away wi him down south an that. I took my HGV when I was twenty, an the sayin is, once it's in your blood, that's it. An I think it's a bit like that. Once ye do long distance, ye can't get away from it.

DAVID SEY, 34, lorry driver, Aberdeen

It's an even stranger thing, this glamour of the fourteen-wheelers, when you look at what's involved. These are men who typically cover much more than a hundred thousand miles of road each year in their 38-tonne giants, doing the same routes over and over, away from their homes and loved ones five nights of the week, washing and eating at the roadside, and sleeping in a bed behind the driver's seat.

Ye do get fed up doin the same routes, but then ye have a holiday an ye're okay again. An if ye like a lot o social life it destroys that a wee bit. Ye're tired when ye get back on a Friday, an if ye're drivin on a Sunday mornin, ye can't really drink on a Saturday. But ye do get used to it. An the lorries are a lot better now. A lot more comfortable, an a lot more power. I've got my own TV and fridge in the cab, phone, CB, radio cassette. If we're runnin wi other drivers, it passes the time tae have somebody tae talk to on the CB for two or three days. An ye get tae know where the good places are tae stop the night, the clean truck stops where ye'll get a shower an somethin decent tae eat.

DAVID SEY

The money's not too bad, ye get quite a good livin. I wouldnae think o doin anythin else. I got married not too long ago, an I speak to ma wife every night on the telephone. It doesn't do a lot for your home life – she does get a bit lonely sometimes – but as long as it wasnae goin to come between her an me, I wouldn't change it.

NEIL CRAIG

The best time in this job is in the summertime, if ye get a wee run up the Black Isle there, or down the West Country, an there's no rush, a nice summer's day just cruisin along down there quietly. Most of the time ye're chasin against the book, an ye get customers givin ye a bit of earache if ye deliver wrong goods or damaged or somethin, an it's no your fault. It's a lonely life as well, ye could say; most of the time you're on your own. But ye meet quite a few rogues, ye could say. I've got quite a few friends – well, ye wouldn't say they are friends – associates, that ye pick up over the years. An ye get paid your weekly wage, an then your time-an-a-half, about twenty-five hours. An double on a Sunday.

JIM COOPER, 33, lorry driver, Aberdeen

But the pay-off for decades of blind romance with the combustion engine is rushing upon us. As the problems of accidents, pollution, loss of amenity and traffic jams worsen by the day, the 'experts' have come to the startling conclusion that building more roads may not be the answer. We may have a long wait, though, if we anticipate them telling us what the answer actually is.

It's not the deregulation which has opened up the bus services to private competition, yet again putting pressure on the people who live beyond the profitable routes. (Passenger journeys on local bus services fell by twenty-six percent in the decade to 1996.) It's not, surely, the raising of the tonnage limit for long-distance lorries to forty-four tonnes in 1997. Or the continued growth in the number of cars on the roads.

Some days ye get a bit het up. The traffic nowadays is just a hassle.

JIM COOPER

The roads have got a lot better over the years, but the traffic's got a lot worse. I hate the A1 from Edinburgh to Newcastle, that's about the worst. But I've not had much in the way of accidents. A few months ago on the Dundee–Perth road a woman came down the wrong side of a dual carriageway. She'd come out o a service station an misunderstood the roadworks. I went into the side of her; but she was lucky, she just had cuts and that.

DAVID SEY

> It has changed, it's horrendous. We sit in the middle of a very
> large commuter web, because o the price o housin. If I had a
> pound for every time somebody stuck a finger up to me, I'd
> be a rich man.
>
> BRIAN O'NEILL, 49, *taxi-driver, Aberdeen*

The sad story is that the cities have been completely unprepared
for the traffic problems which are now threatening to swamp them,
and have flapped ineffectually for years as the dark clouds have
gathered. Edinburgh has long been mooted as an important site
for an underground railway; well, at least a revival of its suburban
railway line; well, a combination of light rail and trams; well . . . Oh,
anyway, let's hear it for the new cycle lanes, and the fast bus to the
airport.

Glasgow remains our one city to stay a little ahead of the game,
for – uniquely in Britain outside London – it has a passenger-carrying
underground railway. Since the days of the Empire, whose wealth
paid for the huge construction programme in 1896, 'the Subway' has
carried millions of passengers every year round the fifteen stations on
its single loop.

The system has remained small through all the eras of wealth
when it could have usefully expanded to serve a much bigger area,
but its advantages in a crowded inner city are still plain; every subway
ticket sold is matched by a council subsidy. And, hurtling through
the ground beneath the city, the subterranean train drivers have a
worm's eye view of the seething urban congestion which was once,
in more innocent days, known as rush-hour.

> Some o the peak times, first thing in the mornin, it's worse
> than a football crowd. The sheer mass o people. Ye come into
> a station an ye're jam-packed already, an it seems like there's
> millions o people standin on the platform, an ye think my
> God, they're never goin tae get on.
>
> MARINA REA, 30, *underground train driver, Glasgow*

The football fans themselves can be quite frightenin, especially
if they get a wee bit rowdy. Ye're sort of shoutin in the PA –
stand back, don't attempt tae board – an ye get maybe 200
football fans in one coach, an they start singin an cheerin an
stampin their feet, an the train does vibrate. There's only one
wee door between you an them. One time at Ibrox there were
Rangers fans on one platform, an Partick Thistle fans on the

other, an they were jumpin all over the track, goin at each
other. I think the controller saw it on the cameras an cut the
power. People don't realise it's 650 volts ye're goin tae get off
the track.

LESLEY QUIGLEY, 29, *underground train driver, Glasgow*

Yet if there are signs of real hope for the future in Scottish transport,
they seem, curiously, to be coming from the one area where the most
damage has been done. After all the mismanagement, there's still life
in the railways.

Keith closed down with the Beeching. I was on late shift, and
I was actually the last person to lock the door. So I took the
clerical exam in Inverness, and then I came up to Aviemore
in 1968. And I liked the place. Ye just had to go outside
and look down the platform right up into the mountains,
the Cairngorms. Beautiful. There's nowhere in Britain ye'll
get a view like that. And it's a beautiful station – all wooden
fretwork and the fancy ironwork and canopies, and a nice
bridge. It was in its heyday then, an it was goin like a bomb.
There was a lot more clerks, an area manager an porters.
There's just three of us now. Everythin's done by computer.
But it's still busy. We get about twenty-two trains through
a day, and after the porter goes home at four o'clock we've
got to do the trains as well – takin the parcels on and off,
checkin the doors, takin off any disabled passengers, as well
as cleanin the waitin-room an the toilets, an snow duties in the
wintertime. An there's everybody comes to the railway station
at some time. Ye get people goin to London on business quite
regularly on the overnight sleepers. People goin to Glasgow
an Edinburgh an Inverness for the day trips an the shoppin.

WILLIE CRUIKSHANK

I remember the railwaymen thinking it was a death sentence
when they were being taken over by British Rail in 1948. I was
just a boy then, but the old station-masters – midden-heids,
we called them – they were throwing up their hands in horror
at the very thought of it.

GEORGE ALLAN

There's even still a measure of local employment, by the tracks, and
new recruits coming in.

I'm very happy here. I can't imagine sitting behind a desk typing all day, and the work in Aviemore tends to be in the tourist industry – coffee-shops and things like that. But this job keeps you on your toes; you're doing a bit of everything. And I'm still learning. There's about 17 million different types of tickets, and there's constantly things changing. And Willie and George look after me here. If they start talking railway talk I still get very lost sometimes – shorthand speech about the different types of engines and things like that, I haven't got a clue. But it's interesting to hear the stories.

SARAH JULIAN, *30, station booking clerk, Aviemore*

The Tories' determined privatisation of the railways in the 1990s fragmented a once-unified company into a complicated mess of overlapping franchises, each with a measure of accountability to whatever transport responsibilities Westminster does accept. Yet it really is beginning to look as if commercialisation is the one thing which is going to provide the injection of ideas and impetus no politician had been able to produce in fifty years.

In the early 1990s, nothing could have telegraphed the attitude of the bureaucrats to the railways more brazenly than the decision to save money on the maintenance of the Forth Bridge. Here was one of the great symbols of the best side of the Industrial Revolution, gone to rust and rot (an insult all the more stinging because the metal monument's worldwide legend hung on the detail that it was painted from one end to the other, over and over, without a pause).

In 1996 they started painting the bridge again. Within months, the new rail freight company was running goods on lines that hadn't carried freight for decades, and talking of the possible reopening of lines at Kincardine and Dumfries. The passenger carriers, too, talk a good game in terms of overdue investment and improving services. The time for Scotland's railways may actually be coming again, even if there's never going to be anything quite like the glory days of our last Victorian industry.

To tell ye the truth, when I was a young lad at Keith, on the Friday, when the last o the steam trains was going, I thought – oh, thank goodness, peace and quiet; we'll not get the engines all steamed up, and the noise. And I came down on the Monday – and it was like a graveyard. I didnae like it at all.

WILLIE CRUIKSHANK

NOTES
1. Anybody who doesn't know who Toad is should take this book immediately to the shop it was bought from, explain the error, and swap it for *The Wind In The Willows* by (Edinburgh-born) Kenneth Grahame, published by Everyman Classics at £8.99.

Livin on the Edge o Life
HOUSING AND HEALTH

Tim Holden is known in academic circles around the globe as one of those experts who specialises in the study of mummified remains preserved in ancient mud; but as he says himself, 'You can't make a living in bog bodies.' One of his more regular earners in recent times has been to do with trying to find out if the Scots have always deserved their reputation for primitive eating habits.

> On the botanical side Scotland is very much oriented archaeo-logically to barley and oats, so it's a case of trying to work out more complex stories, and trying to find out what other things they were eating. They certainly weren't growing things like all the herbs. But I've just been working on a Dark Ages crannog in Boston in Ayrshire – an island in a lake, where they threw their rubbish over the side, and it was preserved in the mud. And I did actually find coriander and dill – so maybe the Scottish diet wasn't as dull as some people think.
>
> TIM HOLDEN, 37, *archaeobotanist, Edinburgh*

Skating round the uncomfortable notion that the Scottish diet may have deteriorated since the Dark Ages, it has to be admitted there's not a lot to boast about in our twentieth-century stomachs. The eating habits developed by the hundreds of thousands of families who migrated to work the factories of the Industrial Revolution – leaving behind the fish and cereals of the countryside – simply haven't changed all that much in a hundred years. If we are what we eat, you could put together the mythical Scotsman with a plate of potatoes and grease (chips will do perfectly), a jeely piece and that familiar can of 'Iron Brew'.

There's truth behind the myth, too. In the mid-to-late-1990s, Scots were spending forty percent more on fizzy drinks propor-tionately than the British average, more on beef and sweets and ice-cream and takeaway food, and twenty-five percent less on vegetables (potatoes excepted). Where else in the world is there the sort of cutting-edge use of the deep-fat-fryer which could come up with the battered pizza or Mars bar?

Yet you can tell this is an advanced civilisation, for while the Scots have one of the worst records in the industrialised world for heart disease, tooth decay, strokes and other circulatory problems, the preparation and handling of the things we eat is a thoroughly regulated business.

This is a lovely job for variety. You can be chasin after mice on your hands an knees one day, and the next day you're giving a food hygiene lecture. I deal primarily with inspections of 540 premises, from farmers an food manufacturers right through to retailers. And we deal with complaints as well. Mouldy or out-of-date food, or insects or things that have been found in food. Nuts and bolts, hair, wood, glass, cloth, plastic, metal, you name it, it's in there. We have to trace back to source, and send things for analysis in Glasgow. Last year a lady had found a tooth in a big chunk of ham, and on analysis it turned out to be a pig's tooth. I don't know if that was a comfort! We have food hygiene awards, now, and a large number of companies do win them. And we go out to schools and women's guilds and clubs and things and talk about public health.

MARIA CORRIGAN, 26, *food control officer, East Kilbride*

Of course, the story is more complex than it might seem. We're not all eating nuts and bolts, or even sweeties and chips. In some circles, as it happens, Scotland's reputation for good quality food is positively thriving.

Eighty percent of the food we're pushing abroad is traditional Scottish products we're very good at – Scotch beef, shortbread, mineral water, whiskies, salmon. In Beijing we had smoked venison, and the Chinese had a bit of a kind of mixed feeling about it – was it fish? When we explained it was deer they were a little uncertain.

LORNA JACK, 32, *Food Team, Scottish Enterprise, Glasgow*

99

Our emphasis is on simple flavours cooked well an served fresh, wi the best produce available. There's a lot o Mediterranean influences in cookin these days. Anton Edelman, the chef at the Savoy, had a tremendous influence on me. An before that I worked with a couple of French chefs that taught me a lot. The French seem to like their food a bit more. Ma first job was in the canteen at Mossmorran, which was a bit different; ye're feedin 300 construction workers in the space of about three and a half minutes with frozen an packet food, an they could get quite stroppy. Ye had plastic partitions, because if they didnae like it they could throw it back at ye.

GORDON DOCHARD, 28, *head chef, Gleneagles Hotel, Auchterarder*

Well, there's a very great number of us still eating in the canteen at Mossmorran. The unpalatable fact behind the contrasts is that what we eat is a dead giveaway for poverty and social division. Supermarket chains stock their shelves entirely differently in a depressed area of a city than in the upmarket suburbs: fewer fresh vegetables, more things in tins, more sugar and fat. It's not even that these things are necessarily cheaper. This is culture, and it's a mighty difficult thing to change around.

It's all vegetables I grow here – tatties, leeks, cabbage, lettuce, peas. I gie a lot o it away. I don't really like any o it masel. I'll take vegetables in soup, an I like the mashed tatties, but that's as far as it goes.

JOHN HADDOW, 47, *high-rise caretaker, Budhill and Springboig allotments, Glasgow*

The way of life which originated in the industrial dormitory of the Central Belt has brought us other legacies, too. Chief among them is a terrible, persistent housing problem. Like a people-eating machine, Victorian Glasgow sucked swathes of the population of Scotland and Ireland into its frantic, ballooning belly until more than 800,000 of them lived within three miles of the city centre.

It was the period of drive and optimism after the Second World War which finally turned up an answer to the blight. The way to deal with overcrowded, insanitary urban housing, and particularly the squalor of the Glasgow tenements, the experts announced, was to plan and build completely new towns.

The diggers moved in, the concrete was poured, and, modelled on the latest utopian designs to combine work, leisure, and accommodation in one community, the new towns were quickly hailed as a success story of the modern age. Today some 260,000 – one in twenty of Scotland's population – live in East Kilbride, Glenrothes, Cumbernauld, Livingston or Irvine.

When we moved to East Kilbride, it was that time when the squalor o the slums in Glasgow was somethin to be avoided. An a new town, it's all got to be stated – right, here's where ye do your shoppin, if ye want to go for a drink the place is here – an space isn't at a premium, so ye've got big schools wi lots o ground an stuff like that, an it's all quite unnatural. Sterile. Mind you, the folk that came out o Glasgow brought a lot of the traditions wi them, like expressions like menodgies an stuff – menodgies is where in a close, if it's say nine flats, all the wifies there will put a pound a week into the pot, an every nine weeks it's a wee windfall, for buyin shoes for the weans, or whatever. In our street, there were the Mackenzies, they came away from Shettleston, an next door to them was the Telfords, they came from Mount Florida, an there was still very much people livin – not in one another's pockets, but such a way whereby they'd look after your kids, ye know. They just generally looked after one another. It was done in a sort of seamless, uncontrived way, it just happened; like ye went up the street to do Mrs McGregor's shoppin, cause she's gettin on a bit ... An I suppose it was inherited from the closes that people came away from.

JIMMIE MACDONALD, 42, *architect, Glasgow*

The new towns certainly haven't been a simple success story. By the 1970s they were attracting so many people to leave Glasgow that the 'overspill' policy was abandoned; too late. In sixty years, the population of the one-time second city of the Empire has halved, and it is still going down. Where the tenements were razed, there are still swathes of dereliction. And at the same time, in the scientifically structured new towns, there's an abiding nostalgia for the vigorous sense of community which was wiped out with the old, overcrowded streets.

. . .Oh, but ah'm longin for ma ain close,
It was nane o yuir wally, juist a plain close,
An ah'm nearly roon the bend,
For ma ain wee single-end,
Farewell tae dear old Gorbals
An ma ain close.
from 'Ma Ain Close', by Duncan Macrae

The move out of the run-down inner cities wasn't only to the new towns. Far-flung council estates like Castlemilk, Drumchapel and Easterhouse on the outskirts of Glasgow, and Craigmillar, Wester Hailes and Pilton round Edinburgh, also sucked the poorest citizens to the very fringes of the cities' life. These grey schemes in the suburban hinterland, often built with virtually no local amenities – no pubs, no shops, no schools, no doctors, no entertainment, no employment – were the ultimate planning disaster. Greater Easterhouse, with a population approaching that of Perth, had no medical centre until 1983. It was around the same time that the Third World charity Oxfam set up their first British project, in Craigmillar.

Like the city tenements, these schemes are the postcodes of poverty, purpose-built. With community-based initiatives and outside help – Craigmillar Festival, Wester Hailes Projects, Greater Easterhouse Development Company – the fight is on to tackle the problems; but against very substantial odds.

Especially when ye start in the job, there are incidents; people who are livin in conditions through no fault of their own, which . . . When I worked at Inverclyde ye would go into a block o flats an they'd look very run down from the outside, an inside, it might be a woman of sixty . . . It can be quite distressing to have to walk away from certain instances.

KENNY BOAG, 26, *environmental health officer,*
East Kilbride

Ye never know what's comin in. Ye might get lovely things, or ye might get disgusting things. We had two or three bags o clothin handed in a while back that had maggots. We tipped the stuff out on the shop floor, an it was livin! We had to spray the shop, an I went home an had a hot bath.

DIANE FERRIE, *shop assistant, Oxfam, Falkirk*

In the late '70s I was going round for the council in Glasgow, to have a look at the tenements to see if they could be modernised, or three flats knocked into two, or whatever. An there's one thing that always sticks in ma mind; a Mrs Donaldson, that we'd had trouble findin in, because she was always away at the pensioners' club, where she didnae have to pay for the heatin. So in the end I turned up an knocked on the door, the door opens, an it's Mrs Donaldson, probly in her sixties by that time. 'Oh come in son, I've been expectin you.' So I went in an sat down. Everythin was nice an clean, but very spartan, an she had this lace cover on the table that had obviously been very heavily darned, with stains an wear an things like that. Well, she was away an brought in a pot o tea an half a pot o jam an that, an that was as good as it got. So she took me through the house, an I made a few notes an that, an it wasn't until I asked her to look at this chart, 'Can ye look at this here, an tell me about your hot water, or anythin ye'd like to be improved, or whatever?' She said 'Oh that's no use tae me, son.' I thought, oh well, she must be illiterate. 'Would ye like me tae read it to ye?' 'Well if ye wouldnae mind, son; cause I'm blind.' An when people talk about poverty now, ye think o somebody like that, that the main thing in their life is can I afford to keep the flat warm, or whatever . . . People livin on the edge o life.

JIMMIE MacDONALD

We Always Knew the Plant was Goin to Close
THE LIFELINES

The process of groping for an industrial base which would follow on from our Victorian inheritance has been protracted and painful. The businesses which successive post-war governments hoped would take the place of the collapsing traditional industries were often ill-conceived, inadequately funded and poorly carried through. None has lived up to what were often desperate hopes.

It's well recorded now how the ailing steel business in the West of Scotland finally won a modern steelworks in the late 1950s, only to find the new complex saddled with a wealth-draining strip mill and sited in Motherwell, far from the tidewater site a modern industry required. A workforce of 14,000 were turning out 3000 tonnes of steel a day not long after Ravenscraig opened in 1963; but by 1996, the last traces of the site had been wiped away.

I only knew Motherwell as a football team when I came down from Glasgow to take a job in 1975. An it was the massiveness of Ravenscraig that got me, the scale of the thing. It was a self-contained steelworks; we made the coke that went into the blast furnace, an made the iron, an poured the iron into the vessels. An the smell, an the noise, an the vibration, I'd defy any man to see it an not be transfixed by the whole process. The old traditional open hearth method was still goin then, an these guys measured the steel just by lookin at it, an puttin in a bucket o lime or whatever. They made it themselves. Mind you, when I first moved in there it was a nationalised industry, it was so overmanned; I once sent for an electrician, an got ten. I'm not joking. An it was to mend a plug. But, they trimmed it down, an put jobs out to contractors, an then the masterstroke – production bonuses. An our quality got better and better and better. Customers were comin in an specifyin Ravenscraig steel, an the difference that made to the plant was phenomenal. But I promise you, the job I had, doin steel analysis, was one o

the busiest, most stressful jobs ye could ever find in industry.
It would remind ye of Charlie Chaplin on the production
line in that film, where he was tryin to keep up wi things.
An one of the things that kept me sane was the thought in
the back o my mind that one day I wouldn't have to do the
job. Cause we'd always known the plant would be closed.
All the shipbuilding industries were closing down, Linwood
had gone by then, an they were our two main markets. Not
long after I started, someone had said to me – it's goin to
close, an we'll all get big money. That's the spur that kept
me goin. An when the final closure was announced on the
radio, we tuned in, an it was the same day Kenny Dalglish
resigned from Liverpool. An people were runnin about, an
what they were sayin was, 'D'ye hear Kenny Dalglish has
quit?' They were that resigned to Ravenscraig closin.

DOUGLAS SILVESTER, 47, *part-time lecturer, Wishaw*

At the far end of the country, there is another name which belongs
on the list of post-war Government lifelines: Dounreay. In an area
of few opportunities, the experimental atomic energy plant on the
Caithness coast drew job-seekers from far afield when work started
in the 1950s. Nuclear power was the miraculous new alchemy of
the age, and the 'atomics' came in their thousands to Britain's
northernmost mainland shore, quadrupling the population of the
town of Thurso, and creating a huge new community which in itself
was treasure-trove to the local economy. Many were natives, able
at last to come home with a job.

I was in the Merchant Navy for nine years, with Salveson's,
mostly in the Antarctic. And it was a great time. I over-
wintered three times in South Georgia, me and another chap
from Wick, and Dewdrop from Thurso. It was hard goin, but
it was a good team. They're hardy people up in Caithness!
But I was gettin past twenty-six, and I thought it was time to
settle down. And just because of Dounreay, I came back.

BILLY DURRAND, 59, *health and safety officer,*
Dounreay

Lifelines are for nothing if not for clutching. Rarely free from
controversy, faced with a measure of danger, and with their jobs

far from secure, many of the atomics even today are still able to hold onto a way of life which recalls the community spirit of the workers in the Victorian industries.

A good majority of the population of the county still work at Dounreay, so wherever ye go, there's always somebody ye know. I go to the Viewforth social club, and the local pubs. When I started here it reminded me of being back in the services, being used to RAF camps.

FRANK CHARLTON, 46, *electronics engineer, Thurso*

I met my wife Marigold on the bus travellin to Dounreay to work – Highland Omnibuses. She was a bus conductress. And we're havin our silver weddin dance at the Dounreay social club on Friday. It's a good club, they do Country and Western once a month, and bingo three times a week. Marigold especially likes to go on a Thursday. But I don't know if she's ever had a big win. She wouldnae tell me, would she?!

BILLY DURRAND

Buses still run through Caithness at all hours, taking workers to the site from the coastal settlements. Far from these windy shores, there is continuing controversy about cover-ups of leaks and accidents in a power industry which swallowed vast subsidies while the mining which once employed 150,000 Scots withered and died; and scientists still haven't been able to come up with a helpful explanation of why there should be 'clusters' of children with leukemia around nuclear power stations. But the second-hand fretting of the chattering classes is precious little use to a man whose hard-won way of life is at stake.

They'd say – shut Dounreay. Well it's our livelihood. I've bought my house and brought up my family, and I love the area. It's taken me back to Caithness, where I'm born and belong to. They wouldn't say – it's all right Billy, we're goin to give you a job next door. That's why I feel strongly about it.

BILLY DURRAND

I've been at Dounreay all my life. An my Dad started workin

there in '57, so it's always been there, as long as I can remember. If I hadn't worked here I'd have to go offshore, on the rigs. I've had a few offers – I've got a few pals in the trades, because there was a lot of people went down to Aberdeen to work offshore. But I can't understand people that can work away from home.

PAT MILLER, 40, *chargehand, Dounreay*

There's plenty that run us down and knock us often. It's quite annoyin. They're not local, it's like – where did they come from? A lot of people now is perturbed about it because of the radiation and the contamination and all that. But mostly the population of Caithness welcomed Dounreay with open arms.

BILLY DURRAND

Dounreay's three reactors, as it turns out, are an experiment the Government can no longer afford. The last, the Prototype Fast Reactor, was finally shut down in 1994, and much of the work on the site is now to do with dismantling and storing the plant's radioactive components, as well as trying to rectify the damage caused by gross mismanagement of nuclear waste. The remedial work is a massive task, expected to cost £2.5 billion at today's prices, and to last for a hundred years. Where else, in the whole of history, can men have left such an heirloom for their great-grandchildren?

We're gettin a bit like an endangered species. There used to be thirteen of us in one workshop, but we're reduced to about five now. And the plan for the future seems to change every three months, so ye're always lookin over your shoulder sort-o-thing. But with our job we'll be there 'til Doomsday in the afternoon, if ye like. They'll need the electronic instrumentation until they put the padlock on the gates.

FRANK CHARLTON

One of Dounreay's problems, in fact, has been due to Scotland's single unquestionable industrial success of this century, not so far from Caithness. Just as we moved into the last third of the century with our wealth-generating industries in tatters and few signs for hope among the half-baked alternatives, the North Sea explorers turned up a jackpot which has not only made Britain one of the world's top dozen oil-producing nations and shored up the coffers of an ailing administration, but also brought substantial employment. And from Dounreay to Ravenscraig via Corpach, Bathgate, Linwood and Invergordon, the economic windfall of oil and gas is the single thing which has made the failures politically tolerable.

Seemingly from nowhere, here was a real boom at last, a black gold rush. And just in the nick of time. With it came a genuine boom town, where prices spiralled, American food was everywhere, helicopters clattered through the skies, and a legion of guest-house landladies fitted rubber sheets to the beds of the shorecoming rig-workers in double-quick time.

> The men o' the north are a' gane gyte,
> A gane gyte tigither, O.
> The derricks rise tae the northern skies,
> And the past is gane for ever, O.
>   from 'The Men o' the North', by Sheila Douglas

And if the job-hunters came from far afield to Dounreay, well they came from further to Aberdeen in the roaring 1970s.

> When I started as a cabby, it was boom times in Aberdeen. We were still at the peak in the oil industry, and money was no object. I travelled all over the country, and ye were earnin more or less what they were gettin offshore. I even went to Manchester one day.
>   BRIAN O'NEILL, 49, *taxi-driver, Aberdeen*

> I wasn't so keen on comin back to Aberdeen after so many years away. Once the oil started, that, to me, was Aberdeen finished. The comradeship o the townsfolk had disappeared, an everybody was out for everythin they could get.
>   ERIC BRUCE, 50, *assistant lightkeeper, Butt of Lewis lighthouse*

To the generation of oil-working Scots who boarded the outgoing flights, 'offshore' was to be a working life far different from the community-based existence of their forbears. No longer was the social focus in the welfare club, the pub, football ground, church or home, but in the seaborne canteen, the roughnecks' television room or duty-free shop, strictly two weeks on. And then the helicopter back to 'the beach'.

It is a different world, offshore. The way I deal with it, it's like two separate lives, offshore and at home. Six years I've been on Brent Bravo, which is relatively large compared to the new platforms that're comin' on now, one of the early platforms to go out there, with approximately three hundred people on it. Ye've got leisure activities in the evenin, ye can do pool or snooker, there's a multi-gym, ye can do computer games, watch satellite telly – it's not all bad. But if ye're workin twelve hours, ye're goin to have just a couple of hours before ye go to bed. During the wintertime it can get really cold, and ye're gettin darkness for a large part of the day. Durin the summertime it can be roastin hot, and ye're only gettin half an hour of sun-down. And it is isolated; ye can't just get up and go for a walk, or down to the pub. When it's busy, twelve hours isn't long enough, but if it's a bit quieter, the fortnight will drag on a bit. I'm going back at the end of August, and there's plus points; I'll be getting two weeks off every month. But I'll be away from home, and I've got a wee daughter, a year old. It'll be harder goin away with a wee one at home. But I know what to expect. And there's payphones on the platform, so ye can call home.

ALLY BUCHAN, 29, *diving instructor, Aberdeen*

On any given day during the boom times, there were some 20,000 people living on the waves in tower-top settlements up to 150 miles from the mainland. And it should be said, rather more catching the wave of prosperity on land, making the giant platforms and their equipment, working in the service industries, or at enormous new processing centres like the St Fergus gas plant, near Peterhead. Here, a 278-mile undersea pipeline brings millions of pounds' worth of North Sea gas ashore daily to be processed for domestic and industrial use.

I didn't fancy bein out there offshore for a fortnight at a time. I prefer St Fergus. I don't get the offshore allowance, but it's the same basic wage, an ye get the best of both worlds with these shifts here – two days an then two nights on, then ye get four days off, an one month in three ye don't have the night-shifts. An St Fergus is a fine place to work. I'm still bein trained, an I'm out an walkin lines at night an findin various things an just tryin to get to know the place. They say that's the only way to learn St Fergus, just to physically get out an walk the pipelines an find the physical locations.

MARTIN TAYLOR, 22, *operations technician, St Fergus gas plant*

The mastering of endless miles of wild ocean as the site of a massive – and massively profitable – industry in little more than months was a frankly impressive endeavour, and there's no doubting that many Scots did well to claim a share of the credit and the spoils. The negotiators of Orkney Islands Council pulled off a deal which found them suddenly bringing in millions of pounds every year from the oil giant Occidental, and there was new prosperity on Shetland (where, before oil, 17,000 islanders had not even had a resident dentist). But the achievements are coloured by the feeling that, particularly on the wave-borne frontier towns which sprang up far from the mainland, the oil companies allowed their profit margins to compromise the safety of workers. The death of 167 men in a blow-out on Occidental's Piper Alpha platform in 1988 casts a dark shadow.

I worked offshore as an engineer for a divin company for four years, an ma last job was on the Piper Alpha after the disaster. I was called out there on the day it happened, an I said – right, that's enough. Well, I knew a few o them that were on there.

ANDY MacDONALD, 31, *production manager, Talisker distillery, Carbost*

With more than a hundred offshore oil and gas fields in operation in the North Sea, and more due to come onstream, the multinationals are turning to the new opportunities west of Shetland. The first Atlantic oil began to flow in 1997. But the treasure-trove finds have been made, and the new fields are smaller and less lucrative.

The industry's emphasis now is on using technology and improving efficiency to cut costs – and, inevitably, jobs. The bonanza is over for many of us.

> I moved up here from Broxburn to work offshore for three years, and things went a wee bitty to pot before Christmas when I got laid off, but that's what happens sometimes. Hopefully a couple more weeks, like, and then I'll get myself sorted out. I got led on a bit wi a job, but there'll be somethin. In March they start drillin an pumpin, an hopefully there'll be somethin else.
>
> GAVIN KELLY, 21, *general labourer, Peterhead*

> Now, you're just scrapin by in Aberdeen. Expenses is almost a four-letter word in the oil business, and the increase in the competition between taxis is just phenomenal. There's a lot of people paid-off from the oil industry comin in.
>
> BRIAN O'NEILL

Oil will continue to be a major employer and source of income for some time. But this spectacular windfall apart – and without going into the vexed question of how the disappearing oil revenues could have been invested for the years ahead – Scotland's industrial future now looks very much like a matter of making the most of our changed position in the international market-place. Even Irn Bru (now wilfully misspelt for the trades descriptions pedants) has abandoned its claim to be 'made from girders' as its mythological roots dissolve into the advertising blandness the foreign markets require.

The traditional industries are passing into history, and their place is being taken by incomers.

The World's Scotland

In the wake of industrial collapse, many of our new manufacturers have come from abroad. Our failures opened the door to them, and for their part the foreigners have brought a new business culture which often includes improved working practices and labour relations.

And while many of us are still in bewilderment at the changes, we have suffered a loss of power over our economy and working life which has been ongoing and progressive. The world's 500 largest companies conduct two thirds of its trade and control forty-two percent of its wealth, and like everyone else today, we are in the grip of the multinationals.

Our success in this increasingly fierce international competition depends on selling ourselves, and we have had to find new ways of thinking about factors like identity and image. The story we tell the world about Scotland is more important than ever before. Stereotypes like the 'canny Scot' – which have previously served our financial institutions well – may no longer be good enough.

For while some of us may be reluctant to admit it, the outside world has become much, much bigger than us. Even setting aside the crucial influence of international commerce, our economy and culture have become inextricably linked to the whims of millions of tourists, while our position on the edge brings us more than our fair share of less law-abiding chancers from beyond. The tens of thousands of foreigners who have become Scots themselves in recent years, too, have enriched our culture in yet another way that requires us to take the stereotypes back to the drawing-board.

It's a Different World
THE MULTINATIONALS

The traditional Scottish industries have faded along with the contrived white elephants which were devised to replace them. Scotland is becoming the home for a new generation of businesses, and its people the servants of new masters. And new mythologies.

> It's a good company tae work for, Levi's. They've got a higher-rate system for the pay I think, an there's lots o perks for the workers; Christmas hampers, bonuses, cheap jeans. Ye get them half price, 501s for £25. Brilliant!
> SUSAN GRANT, 31, *machine operator, Levi Strauss, Bellshill*

As much a part of American global merchandising as that fizzy caramel drink, denim jeans first came to these shores with the GIs during the Second World War. And when post-war prosperity saw the one-time cowboy gear riding to fame with rock'n'roll and teen rebellion, 1960s Scotland was a beachhead for manufacturing in Europe by companies like Levi's, Wrangler, and Falmer. The business became a safety net for at least some of those discarded with the end of heavy industry.

> Efter the Clydesdale Tube Works closed, I came down here tae the estate, knockin on doors. An I got an application form here, an had an interview – I'd obviously heard o the name, but I really didnae know anythin tae do wi a pair o' jeans – an I was just delighted tae get a start.
> GERARD HAMILL, 37, *machine operator, Levi Strauss,*
> *Bellshill*

Levi Strauss is the world's biggest clothing manufacturer, and for the battalion of government salesmen whose job is to flog 'inward investment' here, it's something of a triumph that the company still turns out many millions of pairs of jeans each year in Scotland. Levi's plants in Dundee, Whitburn and Bellshill were able to draw on experienced workers from the foundering Scottish textile industry.

In the Central Belt, too, 'Silicon Glen' has been the catchphrase of the Scottish dream of post-industrial prosperity, and has become a vital economic prop. By the late 1990s multinational companies like Compaq, National Semiconductor and IBM were making a tenth of the world's personal computers in the former industrial towns of Scotland, generating billions of pounds in revenue. But computers have been no answer to the employment problems left by the collapsing traditional industries; from 1981 to 1991, Scottish manufacturing shed 125,000 jobs, while foreign-owned electronics plants recorded a net gain of 367 workers.

And for those who do get through the door of the new industries, there's no question that labouring for foreign employers can still be dull, unpleasant and hard.

I'm a Cherry Tree operator, pittin 120 tae 150 pairs o jeans in nine massive big sort of washin machines. An it's fine as a job. There's a lot tae think aboot; there's bleaches an powders an things tae be added at certain stages. On one occasion it had too much bleach – the jean then is too light, an classed as thirds, and sort of ruined. But ninety-nine percent of the time it's fine.

GERARD HAMILL

Ma very first job here I kitted up the lines; Stores brought the parts out an I took them to the operators on the production lines. Most people tend to start straight on the lines, but I think I got that job because I'm a guy. It's hard work, the targets are quite aggressive, an ye're running back an forward feedin the line. The targets tend to change monthly, an when it goes up ye can really see everybody sweatin to get it. I'm a senior operator now, lookin after line D on the main assembly lines – the best one. Your efficiencies are measured at the end o the day, an ye do tend to compare them an pull people's legs about it.

CHRIS McMANUS, 22, *assembly line operator, OKI Systems, Cumbernauld*

For two years I was pressin jeans on a machine called a Big Jim, an I was awful tired, it felt like it was takin a lot out o me. The hot steam comes out, an it's awful, awful hot, especially in the summertime. But now I'm a quality auditor. Ye take five out of every bundle of sixty jeans at the end o a line, an if ye find one fault, the whole bundle gets rejected back tae the operator. Sometimes it's really quite difficult. A lot o people on that line I've worked wi when I was on it, an they're friends. Ye don't go 'oh your work's garbage,' ye cannae make them feel that they're no doin it right. I've been there.

TRACY MEARNS, 27, *quality control, Levi Strauss, Bellshill*

At root, of course, the multinationals (like OKI, who make computer printers) are moving in to make use of cheap, biddable labour. Our industrial failures have made us ripe for them, and the best we seem able to do is to offer the tax sweeteners and other incentives which will make Scotland competitive with all the other countries in the world labour market.

But the outsiders have brought much that is new in the working life, too, including much which we should damn ourselves for needing to be taught. Companies like Levi's and OKI typically emphasise the variety of the work available in their factories, the importance of team relations, and the opportunities for getting on. There's no room here for the old shop-floor specialist, welded to his work station for an industrial lifetime.

On the lines, we try tae make sure that naebody's sittin on the same particular job for any length of time. They'll be moved on once they're really, really good at it, to break the monotony. A lot o places ye're doin the same thing, an ye know ye've no future.

MARGARET HARDIE, 22, *assembly line operator, OKI Systems, Cumbernauld*

It's totally turned around my life. I came in here as a thirty-seven-year-old goin-nowhere person, an I've just gone further an further. They actually try to bring ye on. It's no just like comin intae a factory an sitting doon at a job. They help ye, educate ye. I've been on a trainin programme for the last year, an I've even learned tae drive, which I could not do.

ANN BURNS, 39, *senior operator, OKI Systems, Cumbernauld*

I'll be perfectly honest wi ye: I was in Clydesdale there for ten years, an it's so different here. Ye're no just a number, the people in management will actually talk tae ye, which I always thought was quite amazin. British companies maybe didnae know any better, it was just 'us' an 'them', but in the ten years I was in the steelworks ye just did your job an went hame. An if ye get it in your mind that naebody bothers aboot ye, maybe the heid goes doon a wee bit. But here, the employees're brought intae things, an it's 'hullo', or 'how's it goin?' at the beginnin o the day, an it makes ye feel completely different. Just fae a word or two like that, ye want tae go an do a better job.

GERARD HAMILL

Gone are the once-mighty unions and their confrontational tactics. Individual contracts which might be privately negotiated, short-term or part-time (and often all three) limit the power of the unions across the spectrum of employment. Yet it's plain to see that labour relations have vastly improved in many areas. At the same time there is both a feeling of teamwork and individual prospects. And while the foreign companies we court so tenderly bring us industry and jobs, something else comes with them too; something cultural.

The mornin meetin is a 'chokai,' that's a real Japanese thing, it always lets ye know where ye stand for that day. An the 'kanban' is the quality control, that's what they call it. The only other words I've got is 'dan dan yokanara' – that's step by step, because ye learn that's how ye work.

ANN BURNS

I know people that work in other factories, an if ye dinnae work here it's really hard tae understand. They think, oh, American jargon, ye know. But I've just been on an Aspirations course, where ye're in teams, an ye get the Mission Statement, ye see what way the company's goin. An ye see things in a totally different light, learnin tae mix wi others, and be more open.

TRACY MEARNS

They're Norwegian, Kvaerner, an they regarded the average workin guy as bein outspoken and abusive when they bought the yard. We regarded them as bein dour an humourless. An we've come together a wee bit. But a culture clash is a dead hard thing tae close.

JAMIE WEBSTER, 43, *welder, Govan*

And even here, in Euro-Ameri-Nippon-land, the stresses and strains of working life are leavened by the same sort of sense of community which buttressed the old industries.

> When I started here in '86 I was a bit apprehensive. I'd never even set foot inside a factory, an it was really noisy. I thought oh, I hope I like it here. But the minute ye come in they're on first-name terms, an everyone was very young, about my age, and I thought – this'll be all right. An I've got quite close relationships with some that I've worked wi from the day I started. It's aboot eighty percent girls, but ye see people get together, they get engaged, they get married . . . There were two just married last month from the factory, an that happens quite a lot. If ye work on the person's line ye'll get an invite an go along an have a great time.
>
> TRACY MEARNS

Standing back, though, it's difficult to avoid feeling that we have dug ourselves into a hole there is no clawing out of. For while we encourage the multinational empire-builders to set up their outposts here, our home-grown businesses are easy meat. We're almost hardened to seeing our latest success story 'merged' or taken over, the company headquarters moved away, and the drain of Scottish wealth-creating talent deepening. The weekly profits and the annual taxes, hundreds of millions which could be invested in Scotland, are sent south or abroad. And the process of marginalisation goes on.

> ### HOPES FOR US FLIGHTS GROUNDED
> Glasgow airport will never do a roaring trade in scheduled direct flights to America, according to the UK's fourth biggest business travel agency.
> Speaking just after British Airways announced plans to scale down its direct service to New York this winter, Douglas Anderson, Glasgow-based operations director at Portman Travel Group, told SoS: 'It's because Scotland's become a branch economy. The big travellers, the directors and top sales people who were based in Scotland when companies were independently owned, aren't here now.'
> Scotland On Sunday, 3 November, 1996

It may be a heresy to say it in a time when consumerism is the god of ethics – but short of some sort of protection from the State, there seems little prospect of avoiding Scotland becoming type-cast as the shop-floor of more prosperous countries. And the hardest aspect of that is that the real economic power, like the political power, has gone from here.

There again, what parochial nationalist would have the heart to dampen the enthusiasm of a fellow Scot who has found this age of global industries opening up undreamt-of horizons?

Normally what happens when these companies come in, they lease a place an use up all the grants for the area, an five years later they're away. Ye know yersel, it happens time an time again. Whereas we – I say we – we own the ground here, sixty-two acres, an that in itself gies ye a sense of security. I'm on a development programme just now, tae develop tae team leader, an then it's superintendent. An I'll tell ye: I'll be sitting at that manager's desk one day!

ANN BURNS

Those who grew up with the old ways, like the men at Kvaerner Govan, don't all see it like this. The Norwegians invested heavily to make the Fairfield yard competitive after decades of inefficiency, retaining a workforce of two thousand men in the late 1980s. And it's not been an easy ride.

It's like night an day, since Kvaerner took over. The first year there wasnae much change, an then they just came doon on us like a ton of bricks. 'This is what ye're goin tae do.' There was nae consultation or anythin. We had tae like it or lump it.

JAMES MARSHALL, 47, *welder, Govan*

It's a different world, an it's been really hard. There's no demarcation noo, we're shipbuilders doin as many skills as possible; complex shifts, hunerds o things. And they weren't afraid. We went on official strike, an it still leaves a bitter taste. They sacked us all, an took us back tae work under the agreement we had before.

JAMIE WEBSTER

We've done three ships over the past three or four years, an we're on the fourth. They're chemical carriers, tankers like for stuff like fruit juices, acids, whatever. We have done passenger ferries an the like, an tae a certain extent ye take a pride in it when ye see a ship that's gettin launched from the wet dock. But the romance has kind of went away a wee bit. Ye're more head doon, an workin away tae keep up the productivity levels.

ALLAN CORBETT, *33, welder, Govan*

Who could not want these last survivors of a legendary business to make it in a new era? In 1998 the Govan yard finished work on Sea Launch Commander, the world's first satellite assembly and launch control ship. But by this time, the workforce which twenty-five years ago numbered 6500 was down to just 750 full-timers. They're no sentimentalists, the foreigners. Why should they be?

I'll be quite honest, wi the present state of affairs in here, ye're no super-confident. Multinational companies have a bad record of dumpin unions an dumpin people. We'll be here as long as we suit their purpose. Havin said that, a lot o people thought Kvaerner'd be here for a year an then shut the door an offski.

JAMIE WEBSTER

It's no like the shipyards noo. Ye don't have time tae talk tae people, have a joke wi people the way ye used. There was a lot o characters, but ye never see anybody noo – ye don't have time tae find the characters. This mob're payin your wages, so ye've got tae get on wi it. I would be lyin if I said I liked the work, now. But I hope tae be here as long as I need tae. There's nae work anywhere else.

JAMES MARSHALL

It's changin all the time. Technically-wise I've seen mair changes in the last five years than in the last twenty-five. It's ultra-modern. They've invested millions in it. Anybody that was in the yard ten years ago, if they came back noo, they wouldnae recognise it. There's maybe a thousand people doin what a' those thousands used tae dae before. The main fabrication shed used tae be teemin wi bodies. Well ye'll bump intae a bit o steel before ye bump intae a body noo. But the bottom line is only one thing: we're still here. Despite all the changes, we're still here.

JAMIE WEBSTER

Very Hilly, Very Wet, Full of Castles and Golf Courses

SCOTLAND FOR SALE

The folk whose job it is to sell Scotland as a base for foreign businesses harbour few illusions about the challenge. The global accommodation guide for multinationals is growing all the time, as more national agencies than ever before chase the inward investment game. And from Korea to Colombia, every alluring hostess wants the VIPs.

It wasn't always like this. From the earliest times of trade and travel up to the Enlightenment and the Industrial Revolution and the great age of world exploration, Scotland was successful in resisting marginalisation in the developed world. The outward drive of church, military, educational, technical and trading talent kept us a position in the mainstream. More than a few Scots went on to found multinational companies themselves, like ICI or Bell Telephone (a company which at its height employed a million people).[1]

Contrary to conventional wisdom, though, the world has become a much bigger place than it used to be.

> From the perception of the United States, Scotland looks very small. When I used to spend a lot of time in Japan, in one big company office on the wall behind the executives was the map of the world which is used for all educational purposes in Asia. The irony was that this was published in Glasgow, this map, with the Pacific Ocean in the middle, and up in the left-hand corner, by Greenland and Iceland, was the UK, and at the top of the UK was Scotland. It focused my mind on what Scotland's place in the world might look like if you're sitting in Osaka, or for that matter San Francisco.
>
> ROBERT CRAWFORD, 43, *managing director, Scottish Enterprise Operations, Glasgow*

So, we jostle for our share in a clamorous marketplace, and we have to turn out our most winning charms. And it really doesn't matter if they're selling inward investment or exports or holiday travel, one of the first things Scottish salesmen tend to do the world over, is dust off our image. The planet is full of people with Scottish connections and notions about Scotland, and when it comes to dressing up to tout for business on the international street corner, there's a certain sort of finery that's been proven to pull the punters.

The landscape is a big part of it, certainly. Most travellers could draw you a recognisable five year-old's picture of Scotland, all people-free mountains and loch and castle. And as it turns out, if there actually are people in this seductive tableau, then what they're up to is the very thing which quickens the pulse of influential businessmen in Tokyo and Osaka and New York and Los Angeles. Where would we be, the way things are today, if Scotland didn't happen to be the 'home of golf'?

> Very hilly, very wet, full of castles and golf courses – these are the fundamental images . . .
> ROBERT CRAWFORD

> The Japanese people work very hard tae learn English. The newer ones aren't as good, it's really difficult tae understand them, but they really try. An there's no a them-an-us. They like goin tae the pub, they love a good bevvy, an they're mad about the golf. The golf course is full o them.
> ANN BURNS, 39, senior operator, OKI Systems, Cumbernauld

We've learnt in recent years how a successful Joxploitation movie like Rob Roy or Braveheart can pump up visitor figures at a stroke – if it doesn't stray too far from the artwork of our overseas five year-old. And what good is an image, if you can't exploit it? It may not be the most exciting sales job in the world, but somebody has to be the teller of tales, even if they're only trying to boost the exports of smoked venison.

> The environment is an important marketing tool in terms of food products these days, and the image of the clean air and the wild rugged picture of Scotland is useful there.
> DAVID TAYLOR, 40, director, Scottish Trade International, Glasgow

I think people sometimes think it's very glamorous travelling to somewhere like China, but when you go to Beijing for four days and spend all your time in an exhibition hall with Scottish food and images of hills and heather – you could as well be in Birmingham.

LORNA JACK, 32, *Food Team, Scottish Enterprise,*
Glasgow

So this is our picture, with the wild hills and heather, and some air. And if we encourage our young artist to sketch in a native or two, there's clearly something to work on – even if it's just a glimpse of our engineering tradition ('Scotty' in *Star Trek*) or an image of the romantic egalitarian (did you know that Robert Burns is the only non-Russian whose statue stands in Red Square?)

Our forbears have been putting out markers ever since the first Borderer nipped south to pick up a couple of sheep. In 1920, more than a quarter of a million United States citizens had been born in Scotland. And unlike many other ethnic immigrant groups, it's typical of those millions in other countries who claim Scots ancestry that they don't stay in indigenous 'Scots' communities, but have tended to follow their ambitions within the mainstream of the host nation. The legacy of our entrepreneurial history may not be as tangible as we could have hoped; but it's far from worthless.

Scotland has a very positive image. In American history, Scots were for the most part not a discontented minority; they quickly became part of the establishment in finance and industry, and it became part of folk history that we are intelligent and hard-working and honest. Which is profoundly helpful in our business.

ROBERT CRAWFORD

The exodus continues, even nowadays. In the ten years from 1981 to 1991, 100,000 Scots emigrated to countries outside Britain, and the diaspora still congregates in pockets all over the world for the exiles' Highland Games, Burns Night or St Andrew's Day. Some would say, particularly when it comes to arguing the Scottish corner, that it's vital to ditch the least hint of Walter Scottishness, and consider our situation from a rigorously contemporary and forward-looking perspective. But the much-romanticised baggage of our history is a component of our economy. We simply can't afford to underestimate the myths through which the world sees us. Heaven knows, there may even be some truth in them.

> Our research has come up with a number of values associated with Scottish products in Germany, the USA and the Far East: quality, integrity, authenticity, traditional, natural – the environmental one – and a craft-and-skill sort of thing. And the interesting thing is how far that can stretch; if you talk about 'integrity', for example, that idea can help in terms of marketing financial services, or selling education abroad.
>
> DAVID TAYLOR

There's more to this than a swirl of tartan. 'National characteristics' are inextricably bound up with some of our businesses in a chicken-and-egg kind of way. The most glaring example of this, the one which has probably caused us the most discomfort while entertainers like Harry Lauder have promoted an internationally-loved stereotype, is the money business. Here's a ribald song penned during the boyhood of the current Prince of Wales:

> He's aye been tellt that the Scots are canny,
> His sources are his auld Scots granny,
> The Sunday Post, the Beano an the Dandy,
> – Lucky wee Prince Chairlie.
> from 'Bonnie Wee Prince Chairlie' by Maurice Blythman

Our financial institutions have a doughty history, dating back to the opening of the Bank of Scotland for business in Edinburgh in 1696 (a year after a Scot founded the Bank of England in London). And though many of the money-managing companies have now moved from the heartland of the capital's Georgian New Town to computer-friendly purpose-built offices, the business has prospered in modern times. In the ten years from 1985-95, employment in the Scottish financial industry grew by about fifty percent, faster than in any other sector.

After three hundred years of trading, though, 'canny' is still the image Scottish financial services like to project.

Scotland has a good reputation in financial circles as you go round the world. Some of the telephone-number salaries which you hear quoted in the City of London don't apply here, but most of us don't feel that London has all that much to offer. It's a much nicer lifestyle in Edinburgh. We get all the information at the same time as they do, and sometimes just standing back from the rumour in the wine-bars is a good idea. It gives you a different and better perspective. It's still very competitive, but I think there's probably a bit less emphasis on the very short term north of the border. There is pressure, because your performance is measured very tightly against your competitors – but it's not like a foreign-exchange dealer who'll be burnt out at thirty. Generally things are much better considered than that. We've got some older, greyer heads – without too much hair, in my case – and in some cases the more economic cycles you've seen, the easier it is to see where you are in them. It's not necessarily just for young people.

DICK BARFIELD, 47, *chief investment manager,*
Standard Life, Edinburgh

You don't tend to see the red-braces brigade all that much in Edinburgh. Generally there is a very conservative dress style in financial services here – sombre business suits, and that. But I think Scottish people on the whole tend to keep their feet on the ground. People in Edinburgh weren't carried away by the boom of the eighties and it hasn't been as bad in the downturn as London.

PAUL SWEETNAM, 37, *assistant portfolio manager,*
Standard Life, Edinburgh

Hundreds of billions of pounds of investors' money are managed by banks, insurance companies, and fund managers in Edinburgh, sponsoring Irish paper-making and Japanese brewing and countless other enterprises in every part of the globe. Some of us are out there with a bagful of subsidies trying to persuade foreigners to bring their employment, capital investment and wealth-generating machinery to Scotland; but there's many, too, taking Scottish-based money in the other direction, on the hunt for the most lucrative overseas horse to back.

I'm away twice a year for two weeks at a time. And I tend to

try and speak to politicians out there and even people from
the newspaper industry. That can give a good idea of what's
happening; economists in banks like the Bank of Thailand,
and then people who know in a bit more depth about the
companies themselves. If you get to a place like Thailand it
can be quite good meeting government or civil service types
who know how the government's going to be spending in
the next few years. In Japan we've backed household names
like Hitachi and Canon; Wilson and Horton, a newspaper
company in New Zealand, and in Malaysia, Aokam Perdana,
a logging company which owns the forest, chops down the
trees and sells things like plywood.

WENDY HAY, *33, investment manager, Standard Life,*
Edinburgh

It's not always a happy thing for Scottish entrepreneurs, to see
vast amounts of wealth flowing out of Scotland to fund foreign
businesses. But don't be alarmed – it's another long-standing tradition. Several Edinburgh institutions first became rich a little over
a hundred years ago, when native industrialists' profits helped to
fund the opening up of the American West. The equivalent of £200
million was invested there in just half a decade of the 1880s, mostly
in railroads and cattle ranches.

But today, though something like one in ten Scottish jobs are
still in finance, the signs are that the tide may have turned against
Edinburgh at last. Government deregulation of a relatively sheltered
industry has exposed it not only to a far more ruthless competition,
but miserably – as with General Accident, Scottish Equitable and
Scottish Amicable, and in exact parallel to our loss of initiative
in every other area of the economy – to the sort of takeovers
which make a few executives very rich and remove local control
for good.

The idea occurs that the comfortable reputation of the 'canny
Scot' may just have been a hiding-place for a business which should
have been pedalling to stay up with the pace. But a tale which takes
root is a formidable thing. And with modern communications, the
world isn't just on our doorstep; from Altrincham to Alice Springs,
from peasants to presidents, they're virtually sitting on the end of
the bed.

*   *   *

BREAKERS BOOST SICK BOY'S DREAM
Paisley CB radio enthusiasts are helping a sick schoolboy get into the Guinness Book of Records.

It is the housebound teenager's dream to hold the
record for receiving the most 'eyeball' and QSL cards
from fellow breakers. And in just two weeks more
than 12,000 have been delivered to his home from
the Paisley collection point.

Paisley Daily Express, 28 September, 1982

Soon after this article appeared, newspapers, businesses and even
church groups in every part of the globe were organising campaigns
to write to the plucky Scottish boy who was dying of leukaemia.
Prodigious numbers of postcards began to arrive, many addressed
simply to 'Little Buddy, Glasgow.' In 1983 the UPI press agency
reported that President Ronald Reagan himself had sent a card to
the sick child.

So, it's a smaller world, if you have a strong, simple story. (Too
small, the staff at the swamped postal sorting office in Paisley might
have said; by this time they were taking out newspaper adverts
telling people to stop sending the cards.)

For Little Buddy never existed. There never was a dying Scottish
child who attempted to collect a record number of postcards, or
any official appeal with this theme. The story is a fantasy, a
contemporary myth run out of control.[2]

Still, there's potential in stories. See, in our picture there; surely
that's not Little Buddy being erased? Now, down at the edge of the
mountains, those new buildings; some sort of modern stuff?

Of course we're not a Mars bar, but we can learn some
things from brand marketing. And it's not beyond the wit
of clever marketing people to marry the two images of a
high-tech society and a traditional society; the two don't
necessarily conflict if we go about this in the right manner.
The Japanese do it, and the Irish as well.

DAVID TAYLOR

Just like people, nations are reinventing themselves all the time, and
you don't need to look too hard to see the paints being mixed in
Scotland. And in the absence of vision in our political leadership,
it's remarkable to see a new sense of identity beginning to emerge
from the marketing departments.

It's much better than selling widgets, this. You actually feel that it's a cause you're promoting – the economic well-being of Scotland – and whichever word you use, I'm very pro-Scottish. There's a sense of purpose. We're running a major campaign in Paris soon, hopefully to demonstrate that the concept of Scotland as a brand can work.

DAVID TAYLOR

Slowly the picture is changing. But nobody wants a revolution overnight. The truth of it is, we've all grown up with that hackneyed shortbread-box cartoon. We could have painted it ourselves as five year-olds. Still can. And like it or not, we need it.

Crieff is a real tourist Highland Games; Lochearnhead, that sort of area. A lot o' them have to be told off because they're standin' in the way when there's a boy throwin' a hammer, takin' photographs. But they really enjoy it. If it was just for the locals, we probably wouldn't bother travelling to these games.

DANNY MURISON, *postman, Burrelton tug-o-war team, Mcritch Farm, Alyth*

Individually and personally, we're not above exploiting bits of the picture ourselves, when it suits us. But anyone who imagines that the Scots might get carried away with the splendour of their identity, should be informed that our history of diminution and branch-economy, branch-administration status make it hard to be too gallus. And those of us who might be in danger of 'getting above ourselves' are quickly sorted by the scientifically equal number which is waiting eagerly on hand, to balance things out.

Oh I thocht when I wore the kilt I could dance from
    Tay to Forth,
Trauchlin up an doon the street, whistlin the Cock
    o the North.
But a the youngsters shouted, 'Awa man, wha are
    you kiddin?
Instead o being the Cock o the North, ye're only
    the Cock o the Midden!'

Street song

NOTES

1. Edinburgh-born Alexander Graham Bell founded the Bell Telephone Company in 1877; Glaswegian Harry McGowan founded Imperial Chemical Industries in 1926.

2. The story is analysed in *Curses! Boiled Again!* by J.H. Brunvand, W.W. Norton & Company, 1989.

Ye Just Have to Act as if
They're Not Really There
TOURISTS

Not even a long history of invasion, plunder and immigration has brought Scotland anything remotely resembling the number of outsiders who pour across her borders nowadays.

Depending on your view of the subject, the figures which show how important tourism has become here are heartwarming, or chilling. Since Thomas Cook led his first party of English trippers north in 1846, Scotland's blossoming international appeal has built an industry which generates around £2.5 billion a year. Some two million visitors come annually from overseas – the biggest number of these from North America – and more than four million travel from the rest of Britain.

Many towns and villages in the Highlands and Islands are utterly reliant on the annual invasion; and all of us have had to learn to accommodate it. The visitors will seek you out if the main road leads right to your door; and if you live in the most isolated spot, they'll seek you out for that very reason, too.

Unfortunately we're not allowed tae charge for visitors, or it might be quite a profitable occupation in itself. We've got sometimes three tae five buses a day comin from Stornoway in summer – ye could be speaking about four hundred passengers – and ye're up an doon 116 steps like a yo-yo. They don't really want tae know about the technical part, it's more just 'What can we see from the top of the tower?' It's mostly elderly people on these tours, an for them to climb the steps – ye get half a dozen up a day. But ye let them wander round the station. We actually have tae restrict it tae a certain extent; we put up notices when we're available for visitors.
DONALD MICHAEL, 55, *principal lightkeeper, Butt of Lewis lighthouse*

I do watch the forecast, an have a feel for what the weather's goin to be like, and if it's not so good the thought does go through my head – I hope there's no-one out today. The trouble is people come on holiday, an they want to do something, even if it's snowy and windy.

NEVIS HULME, *36, mountain rescue team leader and teacher, Gairloch*

It's a very responsible job I'm doing, because if ye make a mistake it can cost thousands of pounds. Ye bring the alcohol to the boil and drive off the alcoholic vapours and ye make the whisky. And ye can only do it a certain way – ye can't drive off the alcohol too hard, or ye'll get impurities in it. And the visitors do come round all the time. Ye just have to act as if they're not really there.

KENNY BAIN, *38, process operator, Talisker distillery, Carbost*

The core businesses which prospered with tourism grew up around accommodation, from the humblest spare room in a cottage to the grand Victorian hotels which reared up along every Highland railway line. Tourism now accounts for almost one in ten Scottish jobs.

And today, Scots can open as many as three bedrooms in their houses to visitors without regulation or inspection, which makes bed-and-breakfast a tempting earner for many home-owners with an empty room or two. But sooner rather than later, whether you're running a business single-handed, or working at a place like Gleneagles (whose staff include flower arrangers, aromatherapists, chauffeurs, sixteen gardeners and a teacher of falconry) the point comes home that it's no easy number, bringing in the tourist dollars.

It's a very strict daily routine here. I might be up very early to cook breakfast if people are going off on a train or a ferry and then I'm clearing up the dining-room and getting the dishwasher going and setting it up again. And ye've always got the washing machine on every day, and doing the rooms out, and by the time ye get rid of all that, the morning's gone. Then the ironing takes up the afternoon or evening, and shopping, or visiting an elderly relative. It's very hard work, but I love it. Ye have to enjoy meeting people, and ye get the same questions twenty times. And, yes, when the final one goes in October, ye do have this great sense of freedom about the house.

ANN EDWARDS, *50, proprietor, Rhumor Bed-and-Breakfast, Oban*

The theory is ye're in about eight-thirty or nine in the mornin, away about two-thirty, three, an back at fiveish until maybe ten-thirty. But some days ye're here all day. Since January we've been quite a busy place; somethin always needs to be done. But there's very much a togetherness with everybody. If ye're workin with somebody twelve or fourteen hours a day, ye've got to get on with the guy.

GORDON DOCHARD, 28, *head chef, Gleneagles Hotel, Auchterarder*

Most places get decorated in alternate years out of season. And by the time ye've done eight rooms, the winter goes by pretty quickly.

MOLLIE DRIVER, 56, *proprietor, Kinnaird Bed and Breakfast, Oban*

The tourist market has changed and broadened vastly in the twentieth century, and the grandeur of the Victorian hotels which once catered to aristocratic excursions has largely been replaced by the battery tourism of the sort of hospitality companies you'll find in any holiday destination – Holiday Inn, Hilton, Granada, Stakis and so on. A visitor will probably experience the personal touch at the silly-money end of the market . . .

We do get a lot of stars staying, and when I came here first I'd be very, very nervous about meeting them. But not now. It's a horrible thing to say, I suppose, but it's really run-of-the-mill now – they're basically the same as we are. Though it is fun to see them. Sometimes they're an awful lot smaller or bigger than you thought they were. And we do have a lot of repeat business, and a fair lot of our guests have little quirks. We've got a guest-listing system on the computer to make sure they are in the room they've been staying in for years, or the furniture is in the right place, or the wardrobe doors can't be open, they've got to be sliding, or the window has to be open a certain amount. One couple wanted twenty pillows on their bed, and I don't know what that was for. And I've been asked in the past for rubber gloves overnight; I think they wanted to do some special laundry themselves. That's what I would hope . . .

COLIN BYRNE, 30, *front office manager, Gleneagles Hotel, Auchterarder*

... and the personal touch is frankly unavoidable at grassroots level, where individual treatment, conversation and sheer idiosyncrasy have yet to be ironed out. It's plainly possible to run a bad guest-house if you've no interest in getting on with people – and yes, a fair few visitors have seen it – but the odds are heavily stacked against long-term success for the grumpy.

> We don't particularly want to make huge amounts of money, and my husband and I decided that we would grow to the level where we would still know all our guests by name, but no more. There's a quality of life that we wouldn't want to give up. It's like having an extended family, during the season. People tend to come for a week or a fortnight, and when people are on holiday they're at their best. They are wanting to enjoy themselves and be happy and relaxed. At the end of each week, everybody's kissing each other goodbye.
>
> MONIKA SMYTH, 43, *proprietor, Ardblair Guest-House,*
> *Oban*

In the meantime the ethical arguments about tourism are cursorily rehearsed in the French-style cafes of the city. But like all the economic traps we've stumbled into without leadership, the bottom line now is – we're hooked. Some of us like the tourists, many of us need them, and having grown up with it, most of us are just plain used to the miraculous legions marching down our street in a way that was unimaginable before Thomas Cook started getting his bright ideas.

> There were maybe a couple of thousand visitors a year when the visitor centre started nine years ago, and two of us workin – one of us to meet them, and the other to tour them round. And Seonag the clerk used to sell bottles through a hatch in the general office wall. But the numbers have risen dramatically. Last year we had about 44,000 visitors, and at the height of the summer there's eleven of us working here. We've got a really nice shop in the style of an 1830s shop, and this year we've actually started charging for the tour.
>
> CATHY MACLEOD, 41, *tour guide, Talisker Distillery,*
> *Carbost*

We had a couple of elderly Brazilians who said cheerio when they arrived and I thought, oh dear. But on the whole it makes you rather ashamed – the foreign visitors speak much better English than my French. An we've had a lot o good nights in the sittin-room with foreign guests. We had a couple o Swiss girls last year an we learned more about Switzerland in one evenin than we would have learned from history books an everything; it was marvellous.

MOLLIE DRIVER

It's Really Gettin People's
Backs Up
TRIPPERS

Not all short-term visitors are here to take our picture, of course. Clothing shops in Glasgow have been taking on Icelandic staff for the month of December in recent years, to cope with the thousands of Icelanders who fly over for their Christmas shopping. German collectors have been arriving in numbers to plunder Scotland's relative abundance of fossils (one of them was discovered not so long ago taking a mechanical digger down to the beach at Gullane).

Our universities and colleges bring thousands of students who will often go on to nurture eccentric contacts between Scotland and the world beyond. Take the British Aerospace Flying College at Prestwick, which has trained hundreds of the commercial pilots who are today flying passengers all over the world for airlines like British Airways, Cathay Pacific and Gulf Air.

> The graduates do keep in touch when they leave. We get the occasional postcard from wonderful parts of the world. And they have been known to have a little word on our company RT frequency when they're passing overhead at 35,000 feet or whatever.
>
> CAPTAIN IAIN DAVIDSON, 45, *senior line instructor, British Aerospace Flying College, Prestwick*

International travel becomes more routine every day, and there are some of us who have particular reasons to regret the cosmopolitan trends.

> What worries me is the indiscriminate shootin o geese by Italians. They've literally shot their own country out, an they come over in busloads, offerin farmers cash in hand, wi freezer buses to take what they've shot back wi them. It's really gettin people's backs up.
>
> RODDY MACKAY, 42, *farmer, Kirriemuir*

The standard o ships an crews comin up the Clyde has fallen dramatically. The owners just want the cheapest. An if ye've got a crew from the Maldives who're huddled about freezin, they're not goin tae leap intae action an do things. We're workin wi rubbish. The Germans are employin Poles, now, an the Master can't speak Polish, an the crew can't speak German. The whole thing's a mess. I was on one boat, the only way I could indicate my annoyance was by takin my hat off and puttin it on the deck an jumpin on it. Another time a number of years back a ship arrived in the Clyde, a bulk carrier – wi a school atlas. I think he'd come up the Irish Sea wi this thing, an the Master was just delighted.

DONALD CAMPBELL, *60, Clyde pilot, Greenock*

Ye won't get a really good dog these days without a thousand pounds, an ye hear stories of anythin up to four, or even bigger figures. The Americans have been comin in and bumpin the price up. Out there, the prize money for triallin is very much bigger, it's more of a profession, I would say, an they can pick up all the good dogs that are for sale. It means the ambitious run-o-the-mill chap has to pay more for a dog.

BOB SIMPSON, *farmer, Duchlage Farm, near Crieff*

I've worked the channels at Edinburgh airport, and somebody comes off a holiday, two weeks in Tenerife, and he's got no tan, and he's just carryin a small hold-all – well . . .

WALTER 'WATTIE' WATT, *33, Customs and Excise officer,*
Grangemouth

Yes, there's every reason under the sun to want to take a trip to bonny Scotland. Record amounts of heroin and cocaine are being produced throughout the world, for one instance, and the abolition of internal frontiers in the European Union combined with relaxed controls of Eastern European borders have freed up the traffic. With its remote coastline, Scotland is a well-practised entry point to Britain for smugglers, and the Customs men who are supposed to regulate the comings and goings are wildly under-resourced.

I have been involved in the babysittin aspect of it at Custody in Glasgow, an I'll be totally honest – I don't like it. It's no one o the more glamorous aspects o the job. Stuffin an swallowin – I mean, fifteen or twenty years ago nobody would've thought a person would go to the extent of hidin drugs in their body.

WALTER WATT

A vast number and range of cargoes pass through Scotland's ports every day. Grangemouth, the biggest, trades extensively with the Netherlands, the drugs centre of Europe, as well as receiving traffic from drug sources like South America, North Africa and Turkey. But drugs isn't the half of it. The excisemen are also on the lookout for illegal pornography, arms and explosives, unlicensed goods and any number of cunning tricks.

I spend a lot o time scannin ships' manifests, lookin at the cargoes. An Eastern European ship comin through Amsterdam or Rotterdam might be a bet for havin a large amount o revenue stuff stashed away, or any clothes comin from the Far East might be a shot for licensin. One time we had a Polish ship came in; and ships have batteries, like cars, an they'd dug out the centre o the battery an put caviar in it and replaced the battery. We'd never have known the difference – but that was a tip-off.

WILLIE RANDALL, 41, Customs and Excise officer,
Grangemouth

I Thought Someone Had Put
Sugar Out to Dry
IMMIGRANTS

Our connections with the rest of the world run much deeper than tourism and trade, of course. There are characters who will happily bend your ear about their ancestry among the Roman invaders, or the shipwrecked survivors of the Spanish Armada. Scotland's strategic importance has brought us the attention of other empires, too.

Not until the collapse of the Soviet Union was the United States finally persuaded to pull out of 'America's aircraft carrier', taking with them the locally prized servicemen's dollars and more than a few fathers of mixed-race children. At Edzell airbase and tracking station, two miles from the Roman Empire's most northerly fort (abandoned in AD 83) there were once thirty marriages a year between Americans and local girls.

Of course Scottish soldiers abroad have had a tendency to make friends, too, and many of them have been among the thousands of Scots-born men and women living overseas who come home one day with a foreign partner.

> My mother was from Berlin, a survivor of the Holocaust. And my father was with the liberating army, and he met her and brought her back to Oban.
> MONIKA SMYTH, 43, *proprietor, Ardblair Guest-House, Oban*

In modern times it's more often been work that's brought us fresh blood. At the height of the industrial revolution more than 200,000 Glaswegians were Irish-born. The men who travelled the busy herring-trading route from the Baltic states to work in the Scottish mines were known as 'Poles'. And the Italians have made a famous history here, with names like Nardini, Crolla and Brattisani scaling a food chain from ice-cream selling through fish and chips to pizza and pasta restaurants. Their descendants, like the actors Tom Conti, Peter Capaldi and Daniela Nardini, Indycar racer

Dario Franchitti, artists Eduardo Paolozzi and Richard Demarco, are known far beyond Scotland.

Our language reveals our links with Scandinavia and the Celtic world, too. And some of our words, like 'gadgie' and 'bevvy,' come from Romany; there have been gypsies in Scotland for centuries.

'*My mother said/I never should/play with the gypsies in the wood.*' And she really did, when I was growing up in Huddersfield. But I used to go and visit the Robinsons; they were at school with me, and nobody else wanted them. But I liked to be with them. They had this wonderful caravan, with the most beautiful glass inside it. Then when the war came I was in Scotland, and I was a conshie, and at that point in time you were an outcast. I cut down trees for two years near Edinburgh, and then I went down to Coldstream to be a tractor driver. But nobody wanted to give me a place to stay, with the pacifist thing. And eventually, in Yetholm, I met this woman, Queenie Townsend, and she was the queen of the Scottish gypsies. There were a lot of gypsies in Yetholm; some of them were real gypsies, with caravans, and some were tinkers. And Queenie, she had a small house. She was a very regal woman, too, you wouldn't say no to her. And she said well, you can come here and stay with me, but you'll have to sleep with the hunchback, and I said well, okay. Though it was not very nice. The hunchback was about seventy, and he used to smoke a pipe in the middle of the night. I used to sleep on the outside of the bed, and he was on the inside, and he had a bucket he'd spit into. And he'd miss. Anyway, Queenie looked after us, and she fed us with cheese, marmalade and bread. And I stayed there for about five years, on and off; I had to go to wherever I was working in Berwickshire, and then in winter I'd come back and stay with her. It was just like home. But when the war finished, I could go back to my painting in Edinburgh, which I had been denied for six and a half years, and that's what I did. I just got into another groove. I never saw Queenie again. There was no way I could go back to this earlier thing.

SAX SHAW, *80, artist, Edinburgh*

But the biggest immigration into Scotland within a generation has been from the dwindling remnants of the Victorian Empire, drawn by dreams of riches in the motherland.

My husband's from Hong Kong, a little island near mainland China, Duck's Island, from after the island looked like a duck in the water. A lot of them came over about thirty years ago, things started not to go too well for them, it became harder to make a living out of fishing, and the younger people decided why not go to Britain. It was still a British colony.

YVONNE CHAN, *33, teacher, Penicuik*

My father was a farmer in Pakistan. And it was the usual story, no work there, and so he thought he might do better here. He had a friend in Huddersfield, and he came over and worked in textiles. Well we had a very good relationship, and I kept writing him letters saying I didn't want to stay in Pakistan; and luckily, in two years we were over.

JAVED AKHTAR, *41, shopkeeper, Govan*

Apchau, where all my parents an grandparents came from, in the New Territories, is an island surrounded by the sea. Most of the people there were fishermen, an lived off what they caught. An my father came and worked in a restaurant in Edinburgh when he was nineteen, for a better livelihood. Most people do this sort of thing, an then once they've earned enough they might open their own business. An that's why there are so many restaurants.

MARY CHAN, *25, student, Edinburgh*

It's hard to imagine what an adventure it must have been, the pilgrimage from rural poverty in a far continent to the urban struggle in a country which would have seemed as outlandish as a science fiction planet.

A lot of people stayed with us in our house in Marchmont when I was little, because everybody was poor when they came over here. An when it came to church service time we just pushed the beds together an moved the chairs an everythin an had the service in there. It was very lovely an very warm.

MARY CHAN

I was twelve when I came to Britain from a small village near Faisalabad. It was near Christmas time when we arrived, and when I saw the snow outside, I was amazed; I thought someone had put sugar out to dry. Everything about Glasgow was bigger, and the language was a bit of a problem in the beginning, and getting around, when I didn't know my way. But I found the people were friendly enough.

JAVED AKHTAR

Glasgow's public transport famously came to a near standstill on the day when war broke out between India and Pakistan in 1965, as the city's appalled bus drivers and clippies waited for news. The influx of Asians had peaked with the Tories' anti-immigration bill of three years before, when a flood of newcomers left the Commonwealth to join Britain's booming post-war economy while there was still a chance.

Many settled first in England, moving north when local industries faltered. In 1950 there were 600 Asians in the whole of Scotland; today there are some 30,000. Now, as then, the majority live in Glasgow, where Scotland's first purpose-built mosque was opened in 1984.

And the city's buses apart, the new Scots overwhelmingly tended to set up and work in their own businesses. It's probably true that an element of native prejudice made it harder for the newcomers to find employment, but there was also a considerable entrepreneurial drive. Whether in the restaurant or the corner shop, these were people who'd come a long way, and they were going to make it.

I went to school in Huddersfield, and there were jobs then, I served my time at David Brown Tractors, and ended up an inspector. But I had this idea in the back of my mind, to be my own gaffer. Quite a few Asian people from Huddersfield had settled in Glasgow, and said it was better here than England if you wanted to go into business. So we moved up in the early eighties, and I got a shop in Knightswood with a friend. It was a very small affair. Turnover was only three grand, so we had to survive on that; we had the boys, and we made economies and saved and managed to get by. Then we moved to another shop, myself and the missus, and then another one, and about a year ago we came here to Govan, a big discount grocer's. The hours are excellent – I had been working twelve hours a day, seven days a week – and I wanted to spend a bit more time with the family. The kids are growing up, and I wanted to take them places on a Sunday and things like that. And now, retailing on the small-scale looks pretty much on the decline; the cake is getting smaller, and there's more and more competition, and I'm looking around to see what I can come up with. Property is one thing I have in mind – I think that's a safe bet!

JAVED AKHTAR

Relative to other European countries, the intercontinental immigration into Scotland has been small; less than one and a half percent of the people are Asian, Chinese or Afro-Caribbean in origin. It's fair to say that our racial problems have similarly been less than – for example – in England. But while the small scale of the numbers has bred a happy myth that Scotland is a land of racial tolerance, there are those at the sharp end who have a different story.

If anyone in Scotland calls me names or whatever because I look different, inside me I just don't care what they say, because I feel so proud of my origins.

MARY CHAN

It's mostly at primary school you get kids runnin about callin ye names and that, because ye're Asian. But they're only kids, that's why. When they're maturer, people understand these things. I go to Hillhead High now, an I've got a lot of friends, it's great.

ASIF AKHTAR, *Javed's son, 15, schoolboy, Govan*

I've had some experiences of racism, and I suppose in a way one sort of expects it. The world is trying to come to terms with differences, but progress is not going to be as quick as we'd like. The majority of kids in Penicuik are quite limited in their experience of other cultures, but I've not had many problems. I think I was just an interesting specimen when I walked in. But I think a lot of racism stems from fear, really, which is why I'm quite committed to RE in schools – getting people to understand that there are differences and diversity around us, and it is OK.

YVONNE CHAN

Arriving in the late twentieth century, the newcomers often found themselves turning into virtuosos of the pseudo-ethnic novelty business in a country which is no stranger to the tricks of the trade. The Italian, Asian and Chinese immigrants who flourished in ornate restaurants serving cuisine which was only vaguely related to the eating habits of the places they came from, brought an exotic innovation to the Scots' night on the town.

But till now, with almost ninety percent of our 20,000 Chinese working in restaurants, and two thirds of Asian families owning a business, the incoming communities have tended to keep themselves to themselves. Today a new generation is growing up with Scotland the land of their birth, with a sense of self-confidence, and sometimes with less respect for the cultural and religious traditions of their parents.

> When I was wee, I didn't really have to work in the shop, I just kept my mother company an ate sweeties an that. Now, I like stackin shelves – it passes the time quicker – but I usually just serve with ma brother. An I get a sore head just workin on the till. There's no young people come in, an ye get 'that's too dear, this is too dear'. I say 'talk to the boss, he's in the back'. My Dad's changin the name o the shop to AAA Grocers, after me an ma brother and ma wee sister, Asiah. I don't mind it; it's different. But I'm definitely goin to go from school to college. I don't want to end up in a shop. It's hard work an long hours; an I want my holidays an that.
>
> ATIF AKHTAR, *Asif's brother, 14, schoolboy, Govan*

This generational change has introduced a new tension within the immigrant communities, and at their point of connection with the wider society. But there is also increasing dialogue; the new Scots have become better at speaking up for their own needs, and hopefully the rest of us have got better at listening, for it's not always easy in the melting-pot. The process of immigration entails an inevitable, and sad, element of cultural loss and assimilation.

> I have been back to Apchau, but because of my upbringin I've lost touch with what it is like to be a true Chinese; certain ways of thinkin are quite different. In a way I feel ashamed, because I should know my language an culture

better – sometimes I try to talk to them, an I stutter an can't find the right words.

MARY CHAN

I went back to Pakistan a few years ago, and it was unbeliev-able. Everything seemed so small, and I found the weather very very hot, it was unbearable, actually. And the carry-on is very different, all this bartering system, I found it a really tiring experience.

JAVED AKHTAR

I haven't been to Pakistan since I was eight. I was supposed to go this summer, but I wanted to go to Gran Canaria with my brother an some friends, so we went there instead. It was great.

ASIF AKHTAR

Cultural mixing is the way of it, then, dying roots and new shoots. What the new Scots leave behind them around the world is superseded by what they find here; and what they bring with them should enrich all of us. And it's notable that the great majority of incomers who have been here for more than a few years feel no doubt about that most crucial of questions: where's home?

I've had another life, but I think of Scotland as home now (although for the first six months here I kept saying – Pardon? Pardon?) I'm sure my two children think of them-selves as Scottish, and I can't imagine living anywhere else.

YVONNE CHAN

I've been up here longer than I was in England, fifty-two years now, and I married a Scottish girl, and both my sons are Scots. So I've done everything except wear a kilt. I wasn't the only Englishman in the Woolmet pit, and there was a couple of Poles, and Italians. But when I came up, it took me a while to get used to the broad accent, like, and the words. Like greath – that was your tools, pick, steel and hammer; and snibbles – a thing you shove in a wheel of the hutches to stop them. And then I fell in like one of their ain, so to speak. And I always felt like that.

MAURICE TURNER, 74, *retired miner, Danderhall*

The National Theatre

Like a parliament or a national anthem, a national theatre is one of those institutions which Scotland has been used to managing without. Scottish culture today is a colourful circus of enthusiasms in which the traditional stalwarts of 'high culture' are increasingly open to challenge.

And it's true that there is a kilted, pipe-playing caricature which plays profitably to the camera-hung galleries. But recent years have seen growing political assertiveness mirrored in a maturing cultural self-confidence. In language and literature, music and the media, there is a sense of developing identity.

Personally or nationally, these dramas are never played out more passionately than in the sporting arena. But here, too, there are reminders that the winning of acclaim, the self-promotion, the pride, would count for nothing, if they weren't fundamentally to do with bringing people together.

Macan Hor
CULTURE

What's culture? Nobody seems able to say, exactly, except for one thing: there's more of it than there used to be.

Anyone who thinks the dumbing of society is a useful topic for discussion should be led away for a considerable period of involuntary smarting. But it's clear that the lines between art and leisure, between the things we do and the people we are, are all wiped away by today's notion of culture. Even the once-high ground of the visual arts, subsidised by fortunes in state patronage, belongs to all of us today. For all sorts of purposes.

Different types of exhibitions attract different kinds o visitors. They had an exhibition at the Mound of the Edward Lear paintins, and ye could stand at the door watchin them come an say which ones was them: 'There's a Lear. . . There's a Lear'. They all had hand-knitted jerseys, an the kids a' had these knitted hats. Ye know the ones I mean, the ones that don't have a television at home sort-o-thing. An ye might have a single guy ye have tae keep an eye on, comin in almost every week, an spottin a single girl goin round, an 'D'ye come here often?' sort-o-thing. But it's basically fairly harmless. Kids are the main bane of a gallery warder's life. Kids see that great big expanse ahead o them an think 'Oh, let's have a run!' An the warder just about has a heart attack.

ARCHIE TARVIT, *62, warder, Gallery of Modern Art, Edinburgh*

Ye gradually build up a knowledge o people. We get students wearin hand-me-downs out o an old second-hand shop, an business people, pensioners, office staff, lords an ladies; one or two personalities, o course. We've had Sean Connery come over wi his wife. I don't think he takes too much tae the modern stuff, but his wife obviously does.

JIMMY MILLIGAN, *57, warder, Gallery of Modern Art, Edinburgh*

It's too early to say that the air of social division has disappeared from the high-falutin arts, but arts administrators these days are finding it a lot harder to justify the sort of insularity which was once a prerequisite of their jobs. With more and more cultural activities competing for state support, the pressure is growing on the institutions which can't find a way of bringing in the punters.

> Ye can be in a wee room just about twenty foot square, an there's maybe thirty or forty million pounds' worth, an ye think – what's in here?
>
> JOHN ARNOTT, 53, *warder, Gallery of Modern Art,*
> *Edinburgh*

> This job is no like workin in an emergency hospital, if ye know what I mean. If ye can imagine standin in your livin-room for seven hours doin absolutely nothing . . . I used tae commit half an *Evening News* crossword to memory, an remember where there was the acrosses an the downs, an then I'd do it in ma head. An then in ma break time I'd commit the other half tae memory. That way nobody could notice. But I think if ye're workin in this nice buildin every day the idea is bound tae occur tae ye that it could be better used. I should imagine we have about a third in the winter of the attendance in the summer months. The trouble is that so very few o the public use the galleries; it's a very little elite group o people.
>
> ARCHIE TARVIT

Maybe it's time for some of the men who run the ivory towers to own up to niche-marketing. But it's a shame; a recent survey pegged nearly thirty percent of Glaswegians – roughly ten percent above the British average – as people who'd visit an art gallery. There are friends waiting to be won in every cultural area.

> Ye'll always find somethin in the gallery that ye like or amazes ye – hullo, what in God's name're they tryin out there? Other bits an pieces ye can look at long enough an ye cannae make head or tail o it! An then ye'll get a hook on it, ye'll see what the artist is tryin tae do, ken? I'm no sayin it gives ye an eye for colour, but it gives ye an idea about colour. If I was lookin for a copy of a print or a picture now, I wouldnae go lookin for just garden flowers or somethin . . .
>
> JOHN ARNOTT

In the meantime, the name for the arts which central Scotland has fostered since the war has become a mainstay of the hospitality industries. Huge numbers of the hundreds of thousands who pass through the gallery doors every year come from abroad, and culture is now seen as an important part of the economy, intimately connected to tourism, local support services, and the 'quality of life' which makes somewhere a place people want to be. Today it's battalions of accountants armed with market breakdowns who are pushing back the old divisive vocabulary, 'highbrow' and 'lowbrow'.

Yet in places where a broad sense of community is important, culture has always been something to bring people together.

Last year we did a series of little plays for our wee festival, the Corrie Capers. It was a bit of a mess, but it worked. It was so bad it backed unwittingly into genius. An I think we should get people like the local eejits goin up an makin a fool o themselves. There's no pretence of professionalism at all, absolutely none whatsoever. Ye know if ye do somethin badly wrong, that's what they come to see anyway. They'd be most upset if ye got it right.

JIM LEES, 47, *proprietor, Corrie Crafts and Antiques, Isle of Arran*

Corrie Drama Club winnin a trophy at Arran Drama Festival was quite a highlight. Okay it's small beer an all that, but they send adjudicators over from the mainland, an it's quite nerve-wracking for the poor souls who're doing it for fun. And it was success on stage, the lure of the greasepaint and all that. It went to our heads! Then I said I'd make a play, and with 'The Goat Fell Murder' it was a case of – 'here's tonight's lines, folks'. It wasn't a complete play until the last rehearsal. But it went off fairly well . . .

JOHN BRUCE, 46, *teacher, Corrie, Isle of Arran*

However the elitists try to justify themselves, the simple fact is that most people aren't going to the art gallery, or the ballet, or the opera. They're doing things that some of the smart fellows with the Arts budgets have never even heard of (even if they do involve musicians and dressing up and respect for tradition).

This is fit-tap music, like a jig or somethin – I think there's
a good wee bit o Scotch kind o music in Country. I've been
comin here nine years, since a wee pal o mines invited me
doon tae a club. An ye go, an ye make up your ain mind
there an then; if ye enjoy the music an ye enjoy the crowd
– that's your hoot.

TOM LOGAN, 52, *bricklayer, White Horse Country Music
Club, Saltcoats*

The musical Country and Western tradition which grew from the
Celtic heartland of the Appalachian mountains and Nova Scotia has
retained a strong following here, nurtured through the last days of
Variety by Scots singers like Sydney Devine. And from the Double
K in Dumfries to Northern Nashville in Thurso, the faithful flock
in numbers every week or fortnight to clubs which supply not only
music, but a sense of kinship which may otherwise have gone from
the area.

It's five pounds in fuel just tae get tae the club an back from
here, but there's no really any clubs roon where we stay. Ye
go intae a pub in Glasgow an there's drunks fallin all over the
place an everybody's fightin; but I know I'm no goin tae have
any trouble here, or anyone annoyin ma wife. The people are
brilliant.

ROBERT KYLE, 35, *mechanic, Easterhouse, Glasgow*

In the 1980s things were a bit low. A lot o jobs were lost after
the Tories came tae power, an things got worse moneywise
for a lot o people. It's two or three pounds for a club night
here now. An the biggest part o Saltcoats people are on the
broo – there's still no a lot o money aboot – an quite a
lot o the people that come, that's their one night oot in a
fortnight.

JOHN SELVEY, 50, *machine operator, White Horse
Country Music Club, Saltcoats*

It would be difficult to argue that there isn't a huge American
influence at work in many of our playtime preoccupations. The
generations which grew up quoting the Hollywood gangster and
cowboy movies which were their escape from everyday troubles
still have traces of celluloid in their blood. And it's a testament to
the time-honoured tenacity of that notably Scottish combination

of gallus conceit and dry debunkery that, whether it's hardboiled Glasgow patter or something even more prodigious, we manage to carry it off. Most of the time.

> In the clubs I'm Bullet-hole. I was lookin for a handle, an seemingly Bullet-hole Ellis was a real cowboy who was shot in the head an survived. I work in a garage in Coatbridge, an I take a bit o a slaggin from the guys in the workshop; 'See that tyre needs mendin? Gie it tae him, he's the fast draw expert.' An the neighbours look oot the windae when I'm goin oot tae the club at night, because I've got on the full gear, the boots an spurs an that. But I've not had any real problems. Ye get used tae goin intae the chip shop, an the drunks: 'Can I get a bag o chips an four arrows, please?' My father was a great Country and Western fan, so I grew up wi the music, an I've always liked cowboy films, so it's given me a chance tae live a dream. At home, the kids are sat watchin TV, an when they look roon I'm sittin there sewin ma mountain-man outfit, or polishin ma guns. But if we're goin in tae the Barras for the day or somethin I'll stick a Country and Western tape on in the car, an they sit in the back an sing alang.
>
> ROBERT KYLE

Well, you can certainly trace culture with an atlas, if you're so inclined. The Americans have vast factories where they manufacture this sort of civilisation by the square mile, and the world and his wife are queuing to snap it up. But this so-called cultural imperialism is only a bit of a complex jigsaw. Heaven knows, it's even possible to distinguish something you might call Scottish culture among the maelstrom of racial emblems which swirls across international boundaries.

> ### WOULD YOU LIKE FRIES WITH THAT?
> McDonald's is going back to its Scottish roots with its first fast food outlet in Scotland to feature Gaelic language menus. Councillors in Fort William overruled planning advice and gave permission for a 46-seat restaurant to be built. McDonald's plans to sell 'Macan Hor' (Gaelic for Big Macs) in Fort William.
> *The Highlander*, 'The Magazine of Scottish Heritage', Barrington, Illinois, July/August, 1995[1]

Is the contrivance here coming from the multinational company, or the Gaelic-speaking Scots? Well, both, as it happens. The idea of the fast food chain having roots is as spurious and superficial as any chainstore ethnicity. Then again, ten years ago you would have said that if language really was a virus from outer space, they'd found the cure for Gaelic.

So, things have changed. The Irish and Welsh have taught us that it's possible to legislate a language into at least a measure of national life, and the revival of Scots Gaelic has shown what clever lobbying of government and broadcasters can do. Gaelic has become that most crucial of things: fashionable. And in its reawakening, it is a different animal to what went before; half the children now learning what was always definitively a Highland language are in the primary schools of the Central Belt.

> I don't like French very much. I don't know why we couldn't get taught the proper Scottish language, cause it's more interestin than other foreign languages. Ma little sister an little brother are goin to do Gaelic at primary next year, an they're goin to be enjoyin it but I'm not able to.
>
> GORDON CROSSAN, *11*, *Wallace High School, Stirling*

Scots-language writing, too, has been in resurgence, with writers like James Kelman and Irvine Welsh finding celebrity through stories written in the vernacular. Touchstone publications like the *Scottish National Dictionary* and the *New Testament in Scots* have discovered an enthusiastic audience, and there are the beginnings of Scottish language teaching in schools. There is a momentum building up, even if it is slow.

> 'The Changeling' was a play that had been written by Robert McLellan for the original Corrie Drama Club, an we revived it in 1988. It's a superb wee play, an the thing is, it's written in Scots. One o the problems is gettin people who can speak Scots, an that's very difficult in Arran! Ye can get one or two, but . . . We did one o Joe Corrie's plays which was in Scots, an we just had to change it so the leading lady had a Lancashire accent.
>
> JIM LEES

Still, there's no shortage of cultural malcontents standing by, like the kilt bores, to damn every possible 'inauthenticity'.

Noo, wha did Hughoc think he can impress
Wi's fremit learnin'? Fegs, wha is't unless
It's Chambers' Brithers, whase braw Dictionar'
Supplied the borrowed words he writes wi' vir.
>   Helen B. Cruikshank, letter to the *Scotsman* about Hugh
>   MacDiarmid, 11 December, 1959

Yet contrivance is part of culture. And anyone who loses sight of this
in some bogus argument about 'natural' and 'artificial' conventions
is going to miss the boat entirely. The shape with which it takes us
into the future is at least as dependent on the inventions of today's
enthusiasts as on what we inherit of yesterday's traditions.

That's not to say we don't have some cultural traditions which
are sustained by the tourist market.

I was workin in the jute mill in Kirriemuir twenty-five years
ago when Jim Johnstone picked me up to play bass in his
Scottish Country Dance Band. We were with *The White
Heather Club*, a national television show, an all the work
was in England. We never played in Scotland for two years.
Then I did Highland tours with Calum Kennedy an things
like that, an then people drifted away, an I started drivin a
van an doin music part-time. An now, it seems to have died
on the television, but there's been an upsurge in the dancin.
In the winter we've been doin a lot o hops – Scottish country
dancin in Leeds one night, old-time dancin in Newtongrange
the next. That's just the way it goes. And in the summer, it's
a grand company here, there's always a few laughs.
>   BILLY CRAIB, 48, *lorry driver and bass player in*
>   Jamie's Scottish Evening, *Edinburgh*

I came from Motherwell an studied classical ballet for
two years before breakin into theatre in the chorus-line
of pantomimes with Stanley Baxter, Walter Carr, Johnny
Beattie, all o them; an television shows like *Thingummyjig*
and *Shindig*, doin Scottish-flavoured dance. It was a hard
life but a good life. We would start in Edinburgh and
tour to Glasgow and right down into England and back
again in a circle. But there's nothin in Scotland for dancers
now. Me an my partner Eva – we met on *Jack and the
Beanstalk* sixteen years ago – we've been very lucky havin
six months' steady work with the job at *Jamie's*. We do

five dances every night – it's quite a hard wee show – an we incorporate Highland dance steps into our choreography, plus our own steps. We design the Scottish costumes ourselves, an have them made up. An I've had a couple of right snidey remarks about the Scottish country dancing, an it gets right up my nose. But I think – well, it's me that's earnin the good money not you, dear.

VERONICA JACKSON, 37, *dancer,* Jamie's Scottish Evening, *Edinburgh*

The Scottish Night which is a highlight of many package tours concentrates into a single evening many of the elements which are familiar to our five-year-old stereotype-painter; the songs 'Annie Laurie' and 'Loch Lomond', a sword dance, the piping-in of the haggis, a solo piper with 'Amazing Grace', a bit of history and a kilt-bit, and a singalong 'Auld Lang Syne' to finish. There's not a lot to be said about this, beyond the observation that these are pretty well the very same elements which excited the Victorian trippers.

Strung together like pearls, familiarity and repetition has given them the bad smell of rotten cliches, and a whiff of it is enough to send some of us searching for that five-year-old with throttling fingers. Then again, how many Scots will pass the next year without a communal chorus of 'Auld Lang Syne', never mind some of these other traditions? Good grief, we're almost authentic.

In isolation the dancin, the pipe bands an the Scottish singin are still very strong in Scottish culture, though some people seem to think it's corny if ye bring them together for the tourists. But since I finished with the colliery band, *Jamie's* keeps me active and playin. And I'm also a judge with the Royal Scottish Pipe Band Association, an though the show here is a package of different elements, it's enough to gee me up that we're performin at a level as high as on any competition field.

WILLIAM GOODALL, 37, *university lecturer and piper in* Jamie's Scottish Evening, *Edinburgh*

Really, there's no great sense that we're living our lives for spectators. Most of us have a feeling that we're quite picturesque enough already; and that there are some things we must do for ourselves, and not for the audience. The entrepreneurs who fancy the idea of

Scotland as a theme park have an awful lot of that familiar dry debunkery to get past. Though it doesn't stop them trying.

YOUR ISLAND NEEDS YOUR KILT, MEN OF BUTE TOLD

Islanders on Bute are to be asked to volunteer for a bizarre bagpipes-and-tartan campaign to help this year's tourism effort.

Organisers have named every Tuesday of the tourist season as Tartan Tuesday, and hope that every Buteman who owns a kilt will wear it on that day.

The campaign includes the introduction of a 'sunset piper', which will involve any local piper belting out his own version of Amazing Grace at 10pm each evening.

Glasgow Herald, 6 January, 1988

The dual identity of our rural settlements – 'season' for the tourists, and the rest of the year for the community – stands as a warning of the dangers of gearing our lives too much to people who are just passing through. What would happen to the community, if the season extended throughout the year?

> The season lasts for five months. And all the clubs and organisations in Oban get going in the wintertime. I've just come back from a pottery class, and ye can't do that in the summer. And if ye go down to the town for a loaf of bread you can be gone for hours, just chattin to people about what's happened in the summer. Nobody has time during the season; it's just – hullo, and cheerio.
>
> MONIKA SMYTH, 43, *proprietor, Ardblair Guest-House,*
> *Oban*

But the stramash of cultural commerce has its benefits as well as its losses, and our confidence in the things by which we define our Scottishness, both to ourselves and to others, continues to grow. In 1996, for the first time, folk music in Scotland was recognised by the main grant-giving body, the Scottish Arts Council, as deserving of some of the same kind of support as the classical music which has for so long been favoured in education and subsidy.

It's probably true to say that this sort of change is also related to alterations in attitudes to ethnic areas and traditions across the

Levi's-wearing world. Among the cosmopolitan generations, the odd-couple values of novelty, and of the kind of traditions and community many of us have lost, are at a premium. The spirit of the age is at work. And Scotland, with a history and size which has given it cultural diversity but also a certain coherence, an identity, is well placed to take advantage of the change.

The recent fashionability of much Scottish writing among the London book critics mirrors a cachet which has attached to Scottish painting since the 1980s, when a generation who had studied at Glasgow School of Art captured the popular imagination with a painting style which was far more accessible than the obscurities which had gone before.

> I think it was about 1984 I first heard people talkin about the likes of Wiszniewski, Campbell, Howson; they really caught the world's attention. Towards the end of the eighties it was a bit weird, people were payin silly money. Things have quietened down now, I don't think it will ever be the same. But if ye say ye're from Scotland, whether it's in England, or abroad, people know what ye're talkin about. An these artists come in here, an ye know ye're workin with people who're internationally recognised.
>
> STUART DUFFIN, 35, print studio manager, Glasgow

At bottom this may just be another form of cultural tourism for the Home Counties, but it's not doing the writers or painters any harm at all. Just as with a hit film like *Trainspotting*, a lively Scottish television scene, musicians from James MacMillan or Tommy Smith or Texas, success enriches the outsiders' picture of the Scots, and our own sense of what we are and could be. Directly and indirectly, culture is where we define ourselves and our common interests.

> There's a real communal atmosphere here, and all different types of artists coming and going – a real spectrum, from an eighty-three year-old Polish artist to seventeen or eighteen year-olds, and people like architects or designers. An there's a certain amount of rubbin shoulders with established artists. David Mach was in for a couple of weeks before his shows. An it's quite social, which is important. We do tend to go for the odd drink afterwards.
>
> JANIE NICOLL, 29, artist, Glasgow

I still remember the first day I turned up at Gray's in Aberdeen. The head of the college said – out of the sixty sittin here, ye'll be lucky if six of ye turn out to do your own art; and I remember thinkin, well, I'm going to make sure I'm one o them. And I've been very fortunate. Havin a full-time job here gives me the chance to get on with my own work, as well as keepin my family fed. An it keeps me on ma toes, takin care of the technical aspect for internationally-recognised artists; I have to pull every white rabbit that I can out o the hat to make sure it works. It's very much an apprenticeship thing; think of the apprentices who used to work on the Renaissance Masters' frescoes . . .

STUART DUFFIN

I don't think I'm goin to be dead rich and famous, but I'd like to keep goin, doin my own stuff. It's swings and roundabouts with money, but it always seems to come when ye're really skint an desperate. Scottish art has really taken off in the last few years, an that kind of trickles down to the likes of me. I do a lot of editioning for the studio, workin on Peter Howson etchings or Ken Currie etchings. People are goin, Scottish art, Scottish art, I must go up to Glasgow an see some o that, instead of thinkin we don't have flushin toilets or whatever.

RUTH GREER, 26, *artist, Glasgow*

NOTES
1. The correct Gaelic name of the Fort William Big Mac is actually 'Macan Mor'. Anyone interested in the McDonald's angle on ethnic diversity could consider the words of the company's first president of Japanese operations, Den Fujita: 'The reason Japanese people are so short and have yellow skins is because they have eaten nothing but fish and rice for 2000 years. If we eat McDonald's hamburgers and potatoes for 1000 years, we will become taller, our skin will become white and our hair will be blond.' With 20,000 outlets in 101 countries already, the company hopes to open more than two thousand new restaurants every year. (Reported in *McLibel* by John Vidal, Macmillan.)

I Bought Maself a Little Cup . . .
SPORT

No discussion of the Scots' sense of themselves could credibly bypass the subject of sport. Our culture is littered with mythical characters whose names stand equal in the pantheon with any giants of the arts: the Wembley Wizards, the Famous Five, the Lisbon Lions, Jinky, Caesar, the Wee Blue Devil, King Kenny. (And that's just a few of the footballers.)

Many of today's other popular sports trace their ancestry to this part of the world. Golf is the most famous example, codified by the Royal and Ancient club at St Andrews, where the game has been played since the twelfth century. It was a Scottish aristocrat, too, Sir John Sholto Douglas – the eighth Marquis of Queensberry – who formulated the basic rules of the modern boxing match. Our fantasies have been fired by local world-beaters in the ring, as well as on the golf course, in motor racing and rallying, athletics, bowls and curling, even snooker.

But one sport, above all, is Scotland's game.

> Just about the first thing I can remember is when I was five or six, tryin tae climb the fence tae get into the school football pitch.
>
> **KEVIN PARR**, 24, *postman, Dundee*

> Oh, I was always goin tae be a footballer. There was just nothin else was as interestin tae me.
>
> **BILLY QUINN**, 30, *quality controller, Michelin Tyres,*
> *Dundee*

The first recorded international football match between Scotland and England took place in Cumbria in 1566. Several Englishmen were subsequently taken prisoner, and one was disembowelled. Things may have settled down a little bit since then. But, deeply engrained into the way of life, football remains one of the handful of truly important things which make life worth living for hundreds of thousands of us.

In February I was diagnosed as havin cancer. It spread through me, an I had tae have chemotherapy an that – an that's the main thing that kept me goin, just thinkin o gettin back tae football.

KEVIN PARR

The majority o the boys are like – football isnae their whole lives; but it's one o the most important parts.

DEREK FARRELL, 30, *student, Dundee*

It turned out my consultant at the hospital was also the doctor for Dundee FC. She used tae come in an say – well, the treatment's goin well. I used tae say – never mind about the treatment, tell me what's goin on at Dens Park! Eventually Jim Duffy, the Dundee manager, came down. An he was great. We just talked about football for an hour an a half.

KEVIN PARR

It's probably true to say that sport brings out the worst in the Scots, as well as the best. In most respects it's like normal life in very big writing, which means it's the perfect excuse to inflate our conceits to bursting point. (Only ten paragraphs into the chapter and already I've mentioned Scottish founders of two global sports, world-beaters in eight, and the disembowelling of an Englishman.)

As our best-loved game, football seems to focus the crudest of these tendencies. The tension is famously grim in any national encounter with England, of course. But the 'beautiful gemme' also stands accused of some of the nastiest crimes committed in the name of tradition by its association with the miserable sectarian rift which lines up along the Celtic-Rangers axis. The pattern is the same at every level, following football's deep roots down to the smallest local communities.

Parochial resentments, personal frustrations, a sense of belonging and heightened experience all converge on the pitch for ninety minutes of a Saturday afternoon. And within our borders, from the Old Firm in Glasgow to remote neighbouring villages, the intensest contests are played out at derby games.

There's a big rivalry between Thurso an Wick. We have separate teams in the Highland Caledonian League, an it's a good crack at work cause ye're always slaggin your results against each other. (But ma wife Pat – we met at the local dances – she's from Thurso an so are all her relations, an all mines are from Wick. An in the days when the kids were born, the nursin home was in Thurso. So I have to watch myself. Ye could say the kids're from Thurso as well.)

PAT MILLER, 40, *chargehand, Dounreay*

In Scotland 275,000 adults play football (in addition to the 200,000 who play at school), making it by some way our most popular competitive sport. Backed by neighbourhood sponsors and fund-raising dances and race nights, the amateurs compete for local trophies in public parks, and the name of the corner-shop on a team jersey can travel a fair distance; competitors in the Highland Amateur Milk Cup might find themselves playing one round in Skye, the next in Kirkwall. And there is still a link to the professionals, and the dream, through the annual marathon qualifying stages of the Scottish Cup.

Ashdale had been goin for years an years an never won the league, believe it or not. An me an Derek an another boy came in from the junior team that Paul Sturrock was coachin, who's now the manager of St Johnstone. An the Angus league is rough. Ye'd be playin against guys ten or fifteen years older, an ten or twelve stone, an it was tough when we started. But within three years we'd won the league. It was a great moment. An then we did it again two years ago. Massive highlights.

BILLY QUINN

The romantics like to link Scotland's relatively humble status in international football to the decline of the street-footy tradition which had once bred exceptional talents. But the truth is, just as football has spread in popularity across the world, Scots now have access to a much greater range of sporting opportunities.

Young guys're no as interested in football as when we were young. That's a definite. I grew up on a local estate, an just everybody played, on the backies an on the green. Night an day, everybody played it. But there's too many other sports competin now, d'ye ken what I mean?

DEREK FARRELL

Gone are the days of the 150,000-strong crowds. And there'll be bigger changes still, as the professional game adjusts to a new, television-dominated climate. Those oversized Yanks checking into Glasgow's Central Hotel every April are the advance guard of the global sports racket as it moves into markets like Scotland. After a successful commercial push, the 'Claymores' branch of the American NFL looks set to stay, and it won't be the last of the sports multinationals to drop in on us.

Whatever the sport, though, wherever the arena, the draw remains the same for spectators and players; the nifty turn, the powerhouse goal, the match seized by the scruff of the neck, the cup. The moment of glory. The making of personal history.

Ye've got to be dedicated. We train twice a week on a farm just outside Burrelton at the beginnin o the season, pullin weights over pulleys in a barrel sort-o-thing. An we've had wur ups an downs. We had seven years where we never won anythin. But we've just won the Games league for the third time in a row; an it's a great feelin bein at the top o the tree.

DANNY MURISON, *postman, Burrelton tug-of-war team, Mcritch Farm, Alyth*

Fightin in front o a crowd was a big step for me. I remember it clearly. More than the actual fight, it was the feelins before the fight – walkin up an doon an hearin the crowd shoutin, an ma legs felt shaky, butterflies in the stomach, a' these feelins. The nerves never go away. But they do change a bit. Ye're able tae psyche yersel up, ye become excited. An when ye get that feelin standin up in the ring an your name's announced as the winner – that's an amazin feelin. It makes up for a' those nights when ye've missed out an your friends have been goin on somewhere, but ye've got tae get tae bed. I really can't see that I could ever be away from it now.

LAWRENCE MURPHY, *18, quality management student, Forgewood Amateur Boxing Club, Motherwell*

I've had my fair share o wins and places in sheepdog trials. I won Blair Atholl in '72, an I've had seconds and thirds. But I don't call myself a good dog man; I like the fun. Though if I was keen I could be dangerous, if ye know what I mean.

JIMMY VEITCH, *63, shepherd, Drumcairn Farm, Edzell*

Ye can get a very competitive person an they're out for blood. But it depends on your attitude. I can't be bothered goin an just muckin about on the green, I like a wee bit o competition. Back in '87–88 I won the club singles, the Greenock and district singles an the Largs Open singles all in one year. That was a particularly good year for me. I've won the club championship twice, an they used tae give ye a little cup. But they've stopped doin that now, they give ye money to buy yerself somethin. So I bought maself a little cup. An I've got the two dates on ma little cup, that I keep on ma sideboard.

ANNA SHERIDAN, *67, Fort Matilda Bowling Club,*
Greenock

Most of us will find ourselves cheering on the competitors at one time or another. A smaller number will be the competitors. (But not that much smaller; 170,000 Scots play lawn bowls, for example.) And many, when we're young, raised in the hero-worshipping crowd and nurturing a spark of amateur talent, will try to make the jump out of dreich circumstances; the gravity-defying leap into the heady stardom of professional sport.

I was playin wi Arbroath at sixteen. Aye. But, I was too young, an discovered drink, an things. Oh I wanted tae make it; but I didnae have the commitment. I wanted it to be too easy. That's somethin I think about every day. I should have gave it a better go, like. But, maybe these things are pre-ordained . . .

BILLY QUINN

A very, very tiny proportion will actually achieve everybody's dream, and rise to the heights where they become part of the mythology themselves.

I'm lookin tae the future. I want tae go tae the Olympics an do well. An one day I'll turn pro. An I believe that I'll be a world champion at I don't know how many weights. I don't like sayin it tae ma pals – they dinnae think I'm big-headed – but I've always thought this way. An it's got stronger recently.

GERARD MURPHY, *Lawrence's brother, 17, Forgewood*
Amateur Boxing Club, Motherwell

Boxing, like football, is a sport where up-and-coming Scots can look with some aspiration towards a chronicle of big-time success. While most of us have always been a little smaller than our English neighbours, our wee hard men live on in national folklore – Benny Lynch, Jackie Paterson, Walter McGowan, Jim Watt and the greatest of them all: Ken Buchanan, who in 1970 was voted best boxer in the world (ahead of Muhammad Ali) by New York journalists.

There are clever folk who paint the fight game as the exploitation of poverty-driven young men who become a human sacrifice to society's bloodlust. But though it's true that most fighters come from backgrounds of no great privilege – and often have to make do with limited sporting resources – there's precious few join the game because they think it's the best way of getting rich. In a culture where a man is rated for being able to 'look after himself,' boxing brings that most priceless of treasures – respect. We've bred champions of the world in our tenements, and the game has become that most typical of stories in a country which is out on the edge: the little man who does well against the odds by his own simple resources. Where do the casualties fit into a magnificent story like that?

> I trained the boys from when they were wee laddies, mainly because it's a very rough area we live in. But I wouldnae be peeved if they wanted tae stop; it's too hard tae do even if ye want tae do it. It's time-consumin an it's hard, an it can cost a lot o money; the boys go through mitts an boots like nothin on earth, which can cost a hunerd pounds a pair. But I still train them masel. The lads here have built the club up fae scratch in Our Lady's High annexe; the wooden huts were in a dilapidated state; an it's now one o the best-equipped clubs in Scotland. An when I was boxin I got a lot o knowledge from Joe Aitchison at Dalmarnock Boxin Club, who was probly the greatest trainer in Britain at one time; he trained John Caldwell, who won a world title, an he even had a haun in helpin tae train Benny Lynch. Plus I had a lot o ideas o ma own, an these are just comin tae fruit now.
>
> MICHAEL MURPHY, *father of Lawrence and Gerard,*
> *47, district ranger, Forgewood Amateur Boxing Club,*
> *Motherwell*

Of course, the fight game isn't just a matter of two boys squaring up in a boxing ring. Just like the football, and every other sport, this is a matter of family, and of community. And just like every other story, the bigger it gets, the more people want to claim it for their own.

> When I'm oot, people say hiya to me, but I don't know them. The *Bellshill Speaker*, the local paper, follows us quite a lot. 'The Murphy Brothers'. An we've got a wee scrapbook, we put it all in.

> GERARD MURPHY

WELL, GORBALS HAVE IT

Well, Gorbals have it. When I saw little Benny, our own Benny, pursue the Filipino, Montana, round the ring, sticking out that gorilla left of his as though measuring the distance between Montana's nose and the floor, I thought what a pity this Filipino is portable.

Benny seemed to be hitting the top of Goat Fell. Every punch was a paralyser had it landed. But the Filipino had all the pimpernels skinned from the row of gooseberries. He was a ghost who would not be handcuffed to anything that was coming from the Gorbals.

I was desperate. My own feeling was that Montana is the greatest boxer I have ever seen in the ring, but Lynch was a fighter. The beauty and mathematical precision of Montana amazed me. But Lynch had guts. I think he won on the last two rounds, because Benny suddenly went all out.

Now I can breathe freely, as I did at the ringside when Benny Lynch's arm was held up as the winner. I felt like the fellow at the back of the hall who kept yelling 'Come on, Glasgow.'

Daily Record, 27 January, 1937

Sometimes, personal history becomes national history. There's truth in the old saw about Scottish sportsmen bearing the burden of hopes and expectations from a nation which has been used to having no parliament to express such collective feelings. And never has this national theatre been more extravagant, than on the subject of football.

There can't be many Scots over thirty-five who have forgotten the 1978 World Cup, and the team's triumphal procession with their manager Ally MacLeod before a ball was kicked. (After the subsequent 3–1 defeat by lowly Peru, the *Sunday Times* of 11 June reported that school attendance in Scotland had dropped by twenty-five percent, restaurants had notices in their windows claiming 'Ally MacLeod does *not* eat here,' and the lone Peruvian llama in Glasgow zoo was being protected by round-the-clock guard.) Twenty years later, after a 3–0 drubbing from Morroco, Sports Minister Sam Galbraith was to be heard blaming Scotland's exit from the France World Cup on the 1980s teachers' strikes, which had impaired football coaching.

Back on the local grass, though, most of us are still trying to make the most of limited abilities and diminishing returns.

In bowls your age will catch up with ye if it's weather like we've been havin, an ye have tae heave the balls as hard as ye can. But the old head comes into it – tactics, and readin the bowls properly, an guidin your players in.

ANNA SHERIDAN

Every year ye see certain people at each of the games as ye travel round, an since I've been doin it so long, I get 'oh, ye're still here, are ye? I thought ye'd be too old this time'. But the teams wi the older boys are the better teams. If ye've got a young team that's goin 'pull! pull! pull!' all ye have to do is hold the strain against them, until they die.

DANNY MURISON

I'm no as fit as I used tae be. The thing about trainin – when ye're younger, ye dinnae want tae do it; when ye're older, ye want tae do it, an ye cannae do it. That's another big regret, just gettin over games. It takes about a week tae recover now. Ma days are definitely numbered. But, I've done a course in football coachin; an I'd definitely look tae stay in football.

BILLY QUINN

It's not just that every kick-off, every blow of the whistle, gives us an opportunity to satisfy that eternal Scottish mission, to make something of ourselves. The draw wouldn't be there if sport didn't generate such a strong balance between the personal and the social;

between individual achievement and the aspects which bring us closer to other people.

It's evident that many of the communities which were founded on traditional forms of work, from the seashore to the coalfield, are foundering. Pop sociologists bleat about the individual's increasing isolation in a world of television and the personal computer. We're living apart, in dwellings with ever-smaller numbers of people. But we'll never be alone, if we like playing games.

For a long time our main support was my mother. She mair or less heckled the other team, as opposed to giving us encouragement.

BILLY QUINN

Ma Dad had played, an when ma husband joined here four years ago I thought right, I'll try this game. An if somebody had told me four years ago I'd be talkin tae you about enjoyin bowls I'd have said ye must be jokin; I'd always thought it was an old ladies' sort o game. But so many men are gettin early retirement now, an there's more younger people comin in. There's at least half a dozen girls – I say girls! – my age. An we stay right opposite the bowling green, an I can look out the window an see if there's anybody there. An people are not clannish at all, ye can always go out an get a game.

JEANETTE HYDE, 54, *retired primary school teacher,*
Fort Matilda Bowling Club, Greenock

People take different things from football. Ye'll get a player who'll just come for the glory – as long as he's got a bagful of medals he's happy. Then there's the boys who just do it for the boys; there's a togetherness.

DEREK FARRELL

One thing about dog trials is if ye're a stranger in the field, people will all talk to ye. Ye'll not need to be on your own for long.

BOB SIMPSON, *farmer, Duchlage Farm, near Crieff*

The boys have got quite a big followin. It depends on the finances, but usually everybody comes tae see them. An when the fightin's over we would go tae the nearest boozer – a big crowd.

MICHAEL MURPHY

My wife, well, she disnae mind what goes on on the park; it's what comes efter. Ye're training for an hour an a half, an ye drink for three, an then on Saturday ye play for an hour an a half, an drink for four. She says oh, it'd be too easy tae just play a game an come home. But it's the socialising everybody's in for, the camaraderie. Everybody needs that.

BILLY QUINN

A Place Under Heaven

Much of what the Scots are today comes from our religious history. Principles of equality, a tradition of educational excellence and an austere self-discipline came with the joy-free faith of John Calvin from the cold shores of Lake Geneva, and they have sat uneasily with Catholicism and more than our fair share of idiosyncratic religious variations.

But the decline of the Kirk's influence has left a deficit of moral leadership which is felt all the more keenly at a time when our once-famed educational system is under-funded and floundering. With commercial factors pressing, the educators themselves seem uncertain about their own purpose, never mind being in any position to help the young understand theirs.

Women in particular may have reason to be grateful for the waning influence of the institutions and attitudes which traditionally deprived them of equality with men, but there is still a long journey ahead to anything like true parity.

And, in a place which is thrawn in its resistance to change, the pressures caused by a rapidly changing world are substantial. An unfocused educational system and a shaky ethical foundation are poor social equipment for handling today's stresses and strains. Deprivation, crime and fragmented communities are deep-rooted problems.

But the greatest asset Scotland carries into an uncertain future is a persistent and unusual sense of community values. With the difficult, long-overdue lessons we are beginning to learn about local power and responsibility, there are signs that our particular resources can help us to evolve a new and better way of doing things – a way which transforms the old ideas about the centre and the edge.

I Don't Know What
the Answer Is
THE KIRK

There's no getting away from the influence of religion on many
a Scottish success story. Presbyterianism itself – a heads-down,
no-frills, we're-all-equal-here kind of piety which was pretty well
tailor-made for pioneers – travelled the Atlantic with our criminals
and slaves and exiles to shape the mainstream Church of North
America. And it was this same church-bred discipline which ham-
mered out columns of Scots to be international explorers, doctors,
soldiers, politicians and administrators.

Even in today's lazy, sunny lunch-hours, you'll hear more than
a few of us let slip the tell-tale phrase: 'work-ethic'.

I used to work at the Savoy in London, a very, very busy place,
an quite a stressful environment in that kitchen. Very macho,
very male, an very aggressive. There was a need for aggression
sometimes, the will to get the job done. The people who get
on there are workers, an the Scots tended to do quite well.
GORDON DOCHARD, 28, head chef, Gleneagles Hotel,
Auchterarder

I joined my first operational squadron, 617 – the Dambusters
– in 1971. And though a lot of people think of the RAF as
the old Brylcreem days sitting around drinking gin, you're
actually trained to be the fighting man with the hard hat
and the parachute strapped on and the ejector seat. They're
taught to fight, and they're very aggressive as well. And you
do realise, being a Scotsman, there are a hell of a lot of Scots
in the air force.
CAPTAIN IAIN DAVIDSON, 45, senior line instructor, British
Aerospace Flying College, Prestwick

A reputation for success in many duty-bound careers still hangs
about the Scots, the grey alter-ego of our other caricature as singing
drunks. (I'm sure other countries boast national stereotypes of

173

fabulous integrity, but there's just no shutting the door on the Scottish schizophrenic, teetering into view with his Christian sobriety finely balanced by the riotous release of Dr Jekyll's potion.)

We didn't always get on with God so neurotically. There were thousands of years of committed tomb-worshipping, stone-circle building and sophisticated pagan carryings-on long before John Knox led the nation towards the creed of self-denial which is still familiar. With the Reformation, too, came the democratic traditions of the Church of Scotland, which have become inseparably mixed in with a broader national sense of egalitarianism. The annual General Assembly of the Kirk has even been touted as a surrogate parliament for an under-represented people – especially when it increasingly delivered verdicts on economic and political issues in the 1980s and 90s.

But to most Scots the Kirk is, vitally, a social institution.

The minute ye go in them church doors, ye're made to feel very welcome. Plus the fact that everybody's very friendly. Ye could go into other churches an some people don't even speak to ye, an ye feel ye're sittin in somebody else's seat. An ye'd come out actually wonderin what they'd been talkin about, an it was a wee bit drab. But there's definitely nothin drab at St Columba's. Ye feel that warm an contented when ye go in there.

HELEN CADDIS, *60, department store cashier, Ayr*

I've been an elder for forty-five years. If ye're in a rural community ye've got to support everythin, whether it's the hunting or the kirk or whatever – but ye've got to support them, or they won't be there for your grandchildren.

CHARLIE DOUGLAS, *74, farmer, Ruletownhead,*
near Jedburgh

My mother an father were both members of Trinity, an I had attended this building from the time I went to Sunday School, did Bible Class, Youth Fellowship. An I think when my own family were young, ye start to look at what ye're doin, an we saw the church as a very necessary part o the way we saw family life.

JIM YOUNGER, *46, university lecturer, Ayr*

The tens of thousands of Church of Scotland elders are an important part of a network which is – typically – simple but rigorous. The kirk session (the council of elders in each parish) meets monthly, and each elder has to keep in touch with the churchgoing households in a certain district. It means there's a direct link into the home of every single person who goes to the church.

I was asked to be an elder at St Columba's about a year and a half ago, and it wasn't something I'd actually thought about very much. The name has connotations of age, and I still reckon myself to be not in that category. But in fact, I'm far from the youngest elder. And we were getting a lot out of the church as a family and as individuals, so it seemed to be about time to start putting something back in. I've been a reserve elder for about a year – a minister without portfolio, if ye like – and just this last week a district has become available in the Seafield area, and I've started visiting the people there. It's a fairly well-heeled area with some retirement flats and one or two nursing homes, and the reception I've been getting has been extremely warm, just knocking on doors in the evenings after work. There are about eighteen households in the district, and I've only met about half the people so far, so I'll hope to catch up with the rest this week . . .

DR BOYD MEIKLEJOHN, *38, anaesthetist, Ayr*

Bein an elder, we do wur bit. It's a labour o love. Ye do feel involved. I go to maybe about ten households, an there's maybe a couple o the old ones I do every other week. Ye've got your own wee district, an ye get in close contact wi a lot o people, keepin them up to date wi what's happenin in the congregation. They're more like friends. Some o the old dears have said to me that they prefer talkin to a woman elder, too. Like goin to a woman doctor.

HELEN CADDIS

The job of elder is only one of the formal and informal ways in which the Kirk makes connections. An eccentric Edinburgh tradition gathers a hundred women under the title of St Margaret's Chapel Guild, a group which provides fresh flowers in the twelfth-century chapel dedicated to the Scots queen and Christian reformer. (The fine print of this story includes the details that only people called Margaret can join the guild, and that the chapel itself sits high among the rocky ramparts of Edinburgh Castle.)

There's a very good guard at the castle entrance who always seems to recognise the Margarets arriving with the flowers. Or can I say recognises the type? Because there is definitely a type. Middle-class, middle-aged flower arrangers, I'm sure seventy-five percent of us are. Some are a little posher. (And Margaret may be a dying name now; but when I was in primary seven at James Gillespie's High School, there were thirteen of us out of thirty-nine called Margaret. It was a very straitlaced school in those days, much sought-after; we were a little snobbier! And Princess Margaret Rose is two years older than me, which I think brought the name to a lot of people's attention. There's probably a lot of Margarets my age in Scotland.) Anyway, I was visiting the castle after the war, and I saw a little notice saying the flowers were put in the chapel by the guild, and I thought – mmm, I would love to do that! But it wasn't until eight years ago I met a Margaret at an evening party, and she told me how to join. And very quickly I got a day in February to take the flowers; and I'm now the February convener, sorting out the Februaries. You drive up to the castle, that's lovely. You waft your pass at the guard, and you go up through the tunnel, which is slightly more fun than the normal gate, and park beside a cannon. And in you go. Well I'm not a very pink flowers person normally, but I try to get flowers with a bit of pink, which suits the stained glass window the flowers stand by. And it is absolutely incredible, I've been there when there's been a horizontal blizzard, and there's still been visitors in the chapel. One year I must have had my photograph taken thirty times by Americans – I was so kind to be letting them share my talent, and the typical sort of American phrases. In November, we have our guild AGM in the castle. And we used to have lunch in the King's Dining Room, which was super, a lovely big banqueting hall with swords round the room, high windows and tapestry curtains. But now we've got to eat in the new restaurant, which isn't quite as special. The lunch itself is lovely – though it's really a bit ridiculous because it's always 'Hullo Margaret!' 'Hullo Margaret!' I think over the years I must know twenty or thirty that come. And now and again you meet them in other places, which is very nice. It's pure pleasure, the whole thing.

MARGARET FRASER, 63, *St Margaret's Chapel Guild, Edinburgh*[1]

Proportionately, more Scots still go to church than English people. But however strong the traditions in parts of the country, and however dark the shadow of Calvin over our culture, the truth of it is that for most of us these are Godless times.

After holding steady with a membership of around 1.3 million since its Victorian heyday, the Kirk began to shrink at the turn of the 1960s, and now has barely more than half that many members. Only a third of those actually go to church with any sort of regularity. This puts the numbers on a par with the Roman Catholic church here, which has declined less dramatically. And still, from the generally sensible congregations of these mainstream churches, a little crack stretches out into a gaping social canyon which is built on generations of dogged bigotry.

A lot of men came over from the West to work in the pits. There was a lad used to say, St Patrick's kicked all the snakes out of Ireland, and they ended up at the Woolmet. He was a bit of a boy for the Catholics. He didn't like them.

MAURICE TURNER, 74, *retired miner, Danderhall*

There was no policy about housin people in sectarian terms in Glasgow. It was just that people identified with areas, just like ghettos; an that's why Maryhill was almost exclusively Catholic, as was Gorbals, an Bridgeton was almost exclusively Protestant. When we moved out from Bridgeton to East Kilbride, there was Catholics stayed up the road from us. But we didn't really have anythin to do wi them. We'd have a wee experiment about playin football wi them, but they went to different schools an that. They were Catholics, an we were Proddies, an that was that. We never fought them, because they were on our street. We'd fight the guys from St Kenneth's; but not them, because we'd actually have to live beside them.

JIMMIE MACDONALD, 42, *architect, Glasgow*

The Kirk and Catholicism are only the biggest of the churches which polarise conflict. Successive Reformations, Secessions, Disruptions and other breakaway shenanigans have turned up Frees, Wee Frees, Piskies, and any number of alternatives to the mainstream. Many of them, too, are gone now; Scotland is littered with handsome and derelict church buildings which are being converted into homes, or galleries, or restaurants. And as the diminished Church of Scotland regroups and rationalises its internal resources, its congregations are being forced to amalgamate.

Sometimes the retreat has turned up a new vitality. St Columba's Parish Church in the south side of Ayr resulted from the amalgamation of three local churches in 1981, and its membership has grown steadily to the point where it is now one of the largest churches in Scotland.

It is disquieting that membership of the Kirk is falling, but I don't know what the answer is. I do worry about young folk in general, because things have changed. But maybe every generation worries. And I think we've been very lucky at St Columba's. We had an excellent minister when the amalgamation went through, and in a sense it was something which was born again. In fact the church is maybe too big now. The numbers were about 1260 when we amalgamated and everything settled down, and now it's over 2000. If we were running a business, we might have said, well, perhaps we could have opened a branch office. But we're now looking for an associate minister, simply because the pastoral demands are high on one full-time minister. So in a sense we are opening a branch office, in the same building.

JIM YOUNGER

There's vigour, too, in the faiths which our incomers have brought.

Friday is our religious day, and I always try to go to the mosque on a Friday. We don't want to lose the religion. We sent the kids when they were younger to a local friend's house to learn the Koran, at least to retain some of our culture and religion. Religion is a strong hold on us as a family.

JAVED AKHTAR, 41, *shopkeeper, Govan*

The members of the True Jesus Church – who each give a tenth of their income to the church – are predominantly from the little Hong Kong island of Apchau; a family in blood, as well as spirit. But as this charismatic evangelical group grows, more and more of its congregation are Scottish-born. Services in Cantonese now feature simultaneous English translation.

The True Jesus Church originated from China in 1917, and gradually spread. Now it's throughout the world. There's two in Edinburgh, and there's one in Elgin, which started in the basement of a restaurant. In the village where my family came from they all believed in the True Jesus Church. We have preachers come over from Taiwan or Hong Kong and visit us.

MARY CHAN, 25, *student, Edinburgh*

Our founder was a disillusioned Baptist in China, and our sacraments are different to the Church of Scotland, but I think we're nearer to them than to Catholicism. When you hear 300 or 400 people in the church kneeling down and speaking in tongues, the sound can be quite overwhelming; but it's not as though we're in a trance or anything. Speaking in a language which you yourself don't understand is a way of receiving the Holy Spirit. We have baptisms three or four times a year for babies and older people, which is total immersion in a living body of water, so we go down to Portobello. And we use unleavened bread and fresh grape juice for Holy Communion (we buy grapes, and fortunately we have one of those Kenwood machines, which is marvellous).

YVONNE CHAN, 33, *teacher, Penicuik*

On the whole, though, it would take a deal of doctoring the picture to make Scotland's spiritual health look rosy. And while the social and spiritual services of a national church may be missed, the outstanding question posed by God's decline is – where does our morality come from? At bottom, whatever our faith or faithlessness, most of our sense of what's right or wrong is probably inherited from the Christian tradition.

But if we're not sure about morality these days, we don't go to the Bible. We go to a bioethics advisory commission.

CLINTON'S CONCERN ON CLONES
President Clinton, reacting to the news that scientists in Scotland have produced the world's first clone of an adult animal, has asked a bioethics advisory commission to review the implications for human beings.
White House press secretary Mike McCurry said

the commission was asked to report back in ninety
days . . .

McCurry said Clinton asked the commission to
review 'the ethical and legal issues associated with
this development in technology' which he called
'startling'.

Reuters, 24 February, 1997

NOTES

1. James Gillespie's was the 'crème de la crème' school fictionalised in Muriel
Spark's *The Prime of Miss Jean Brodie*.

Ye See That Many Cheeky Weans
THE YOUNG

The influence of the Kirk may have faded, but who could be sorry that children today don't fear God or the bogeyman?

> POLICE HAD TO CLEAR 'VAMPIRE' HUNTERS
> Householders in Caledonia Road, Glasgow, phoned the police last night to complain of the clamour raised by hundreds of children swarming into the Southern Necropolis to track down and slay a 'vampire with iron teeth.'
> The 'vampire,' according to the children, was credited with killing and eating 'two wee boys.'
> They came from all over Hutchesontown. Some were so young they could scarcely walk, but most were armed with sticks or stones prepared to do battle with the menace.
>
> *The Bulletin*, Glasgow, 24 September, 1954

Here's a watershed in Scottish youth culture, the revenge of hundreds of children for generations of parents' cruel horror stories. The nastiest cruelty of all, though, was in the fact that the myth had originally grown up around an actual local woman whose dentist had left her with prominent metallic fixings on her teeth a hundred years before.[1]

But kids today are as likely to go hunting down the ogres as cower under the blankets in terror. Children have 'rights,' an inconceivable idea a few years ago, and a deal more protection than they used to from the adults who could exploit or abuse them. Many, many children have vastly more money than their parents did a generation ago, and our High Streets are packed with professionals waiting to relieve them of it.

> It's very difficult now getting junior staff. Hairdressing's always been very poorly paid, an I think kids get a lot more money now, an they're just not prepared to go into it.
>
> ALEX ALLAN, 33, *hairdresser, Birnam*

All the same, after school, or at the weekend, or in the holidays, all the computers or the CD players or the TVs in the world won't cure the boredom.

> We go down the street where there's the shops and hang around there. There's the chip shop, and the market cross bang in the middle of the street, and people just sit and talk. Or there's the community centre where there's pool and things, or swimming. And I go to stay with one of my friends in Yell quite a lot at weekends. There's the youth club there, and discos, and a shop.
>
> SARA FOX, *13*, *Shetland*

> On a Friday we go to the community centre in Fallin, or play games an that, an watch videos. Sometimes we go up the toon an go to the pictures. But school holidays are borin, once ye've been your holiday. At least the Christmas holidays are not so long.
>
> TRACEY BLEVINS, *12*, *Fallin*

> Mostly we jus play football. Sometimes me an ma friend go up to King's Park, jus to go an find golf balls, because I quite like golf balls. At one time we had just under sixty, but now we've jus got about twelve. We were hopin to sell them, but we only sold about fifty.
>
> GORDON CROSSAN, *11*, *Wallace High School, Stirling*

Teachers and some parents will tell you that the disappearance of the harsh disciplines of the past has left children more difficult to control. At school, even the clothing is no longer uniform.

> Ye're not meant to wear things like jeans and shell-suits. But ye don't really want to wear some o your stuff in school, cause then there's nothin special about it. I jus wear a sweatshirt and a pair o school trousers.
>
> GORDON CROSSAN

'Kids today,' of course, has been a disapproving mantra ever since adults stopped sending children down the mines. 'They've less respect.' This may be true, but the best thing you can say about respect these days is that on the whole, it has to be earned by all of us.

Something's not working, somewhere.

The kids are a problem. Graffiti, an everythin. Ye see them down here at night on their own. An ye get them train-jumpin, jumpin out o one train an across the platform an onto the other. Well, their mother should know where they are, instead o them bein down here annoyin us.

GILL FERGUSON, 28, *underground train driver, Glasgow*

I stay next to the school, an there's that many people walkin roun ... They're always walkin roun the street an bein totally stupid, an vandalisin the house sometimes. One day the number o the house was torn off.

GORDON CROSSAN

There's an awful problem with vandalism here, kids just breakin greenhouses for the hell of it, liftin your produce an scatterin it all over the place. I think that's why a lot o the plots look quite ramshackle. People've had tae barricade themselves in, tae keep people out.

REBECCA BROWN, 45, *legal office assistant, Budhill and Springboig allotments, Glasgow*

Ye see that many cheeky weans the now, an there's that many bad ones about. There's got tae be discipline. But I'm pleased wi Jim an Ashley. I brought them up that they're never really cheeky tae an adult. But I'm no one o these overbearin mothers that's pushin their kids tae do everythin they hadnae done when they were younger. As far as I'm concerned I'd like them tae do their best tae their ain capabilities, an jus grow up happy enough.

PAULINE MONTGOMERY, 25, *Possilpark, Glasgow*

God and teachers were inextricably linked ever since Columba first paddled over from Ulster. And there really was an equality of opportunity unparalleled in Europe for several hundred years, albeit under the funless tyranny of the dominie. The laird's son and the ploughman's son sat together, and in 1864, one in 205 of them went to secondary school. (In England, the figure was one in 1300.)

But the church which moulded more than a century of Scottish heroes, from Mungo Park (who mapped the upper Niger in 1795) to Eric Liddell (Olympic 400 metres champion, 1924) plays little part in the lives of most Scottish children these days. School has become altogether a more confrontational, troubled and cynical affair. More fun, too.

Oor wee school's the best wee school
The best wee school in Glesca.
A that's wrang wi oor wee school's
The baldy wee heidmaister.
He goes tae the pub on a Saturday night,
He goes tae the Church on Sunday,
And prays tae the Lord tae gie him strength
Tae belt the weans on Monday.

Street song

Some o ma friends call me 'Stevie-dose'. I don't know why.
I wish they wouldn't, cause it sounds stupid. But everybody
knows ma brother, he's in third year, so they go – are you
David Russell's brother? I say – yeah, I am, unfortunately.
Some o them come round to ma house, an they play with ma
computer. But some o them are okay.

STEVEN RUSSELL, 11, Wallace High School, Stirling

School's good fun. But it takes up a lot o time.

GORDON CROSSAN

I couldn't wait to get to school. Ma first day at primary school
I was sayin to ma mother: 'What're all the kids cryin for . . . ?'

TRACEY BLEVINS

A hundred years ago, these 'first-years' would have been reaching the
end of their school lives. But the official leaving age has risen through
the century, reaching sixteen in 1972. Now there's close to 850,000
Scots in school, and Scotland's reputation in the field is hanging on
the shakiest of nails.

There's been a flurry of upheavals in the last decade, and the painful reforms of exams and courses still don't seem to have produced a
successful pattern for the future. The changes have mirrored a similar
turmoil in England, heightening the impression of an underfunded,
floundering and demoralised business. In 1997 a committee chaired
by Chris Whatley of Dundee University revealed that – quite possibly
uniquely in the world – young Scots can pass right through the
education system today without learning any of their own country's
history at all.

The one long-standing tradition which seems to have weathered
the educators' fads – the English system may even be leaning our
way – is the principle of an all-round education, as distinct from
early specialisation.

This is more excitin than primary school, cause ye're doin different subjects. Some o them ye've never even heard of before, like RE. Classics is probly ma favourite. Ye get told old stories from Greece and Roman things, with people like Zeus, like in Clash o the Titans an that. (It's gettin quite near Christmas, an Mrs Jennings lets us watch videos in the last couple o weeks).

GORDON CROSSAN

This breadth of subjects persists even into colleges and universities; only in the third and fourth years of their degree course will most students concentrate on the one or two subjects in which they will graduate. Further education has become the choice of vastly more school-leavers, too. Around forty-three percent of them, now, will go on to further study. This is nearly double the number of fifteen years ago, and an unprecedented change in our culture.

There's no question, either, that student life can be a gift and a boon to many young people.

I love it here – I don't want to leave! But I know I'm a member of this place forever, an I've got all ma photographs, an I'll spend hours goin over them, an I'll keep in touch with all ma friends. I do think of it as ma home, now. It's small enough that it's still a community; ye're sittin in your room and ye know that ye're surrounded by 200 people who'd be happy if ye turned up for coffee in ten minutes. An I do think the traditions at St Andrews are wonderful. On Sundays we have a big lunch in the Hall where ye wear your gown an say Latin grace, an a formal meal is served an everythin. I'm very disappointed that they're phasin some of it out – changing the terms to semesters, terrible! – cause there's a character to it, it sets St Andrews apart from everythin else. It sounds terrible, but I suppose it's a kind o bondin sort-o-thing: ye're all part of the same thing. When I'm back in Livingston I sit an say to ma Dad – I'm goin home next week. He's lost! But I go roun the local shoppin centre, an I can't believe these people, wanderin round and round pushin prams and discussin soap opera an football. There's people I was at school with, standin there with two kids. I don't feel part of that environment now.

MOIRA SINCLAIR, 23, *student, St Andrews University*

It's a bit of a culture shock comin here from a place like Ardrossan. There's people from all over the world, an a large number of English public-school types that are sort of Oxbridge rejects. But the way I see it is ye're goin to meet these people anyway, an better meetin them in a social context an gettin used to them. An St Andrews is a gorgeous town, it really is. Ardrossan is not exactly a very posh area at the moment, there's a lot of street violence an various other things, an when I come here it's just so peaceful. A lot o ma friends left school to get jobs that just weren't there, an I came here with the realisation that a degree would be pretty useful for what I would like to do in the end – a job in the financial sector, or maybe now a PhD. With some of ma friends now at home it's very awkward, because they have a different life, an I have a different life. An when ye're away from home at a place like St Andrews, ye do change.

CAMPBELL COWIE, 21, *student, St Andrews University*

It's an unhappy state of affairs that the dramatic increase in the numbers making this leap into a new world doesn't seem to have made the slightest difference to the strong sense of social division attached to it. Part of the trouble is this strange idea of education being for the young, which means an exclusive concentration of people in small areas at exactly the same stage of their lives. This is slowly beginning to change, as a greater number of older students filter into the colleges and universities. But everybody's still conscious of the 'town and gown' divide, whether you're in Ardrossan, or a place like St Andrews, where the university has been the biggest employer for nearly six centuries, and half the students are English.

A lot of the local people are employed here, an it tends to be the older generation. My grandfather was a night-watchman at the university for a considerable amount of time, so I have seen the town from the other side, an I can certainly sympathise wi the younger locals. I'd hate to think what it would be like if there was a university in Arbroath, where I'm from. But there's not a lot of town-gown trouble; ye tend to find people keep themselves to themselves.

ANDREW COULL, 20, *student, St Andrews University*

Maybe the higher education boom isn't quite the cultural revolution it first appears. There are new universities all over the place, but the proportion of first-degree graduates going into full-time employment has dropped sharply over exactly the same time as the student population has increased. (In 1989–90, fifty-four percent of university graduates and eighty-seven percent from colleges were walking into jobs; as the student population mushroomed, the percentages dropped to forty-five percent and thirty-seven percent in just four years.)

Well, you might say, all these new students might not get a job, but at least they're getting an education. But from 1990 to 1997 alone, government spending per student in Scotland fell from £6500 to £4500. If students are getting anything like as good an education as they were fifteen years ago, it's in complete defiance of the circumstances.

But there's no need to tell students about hard times.

I know there's the image of students, the social life an all the rest of it, but the problem these days is money. Ye've got to keep your eye on the pennies, an if ye're unfortunate enough not to get a job for the summer, ye've really got to watch it.

CAMPBELL COWIE

There is hardship here. I'm one of the very few who isn't highly in debt.

ANDREW COULL

It used to be more the elderly that did cleaning, whereas now ye get young ones about eighteen doing it, and students. Ye know what like it is now; it's hard for anyone to get a job, and I think students, they might not be that happy, but they think, at least I've got a job.

CATHERINE ALLAN, *51, office cleaner, Inverness*

NOTES

1. The urban folklore is traced by Sandy Hobbs and David Cornwell in *Perspectives on Contemporary Legend*, volume 3, Sheffield Academic Press, 1988.

They Just Don't Think It's a Male Thing to Do
WOMEN

Looking out from the room with the blue wallpaper, I feel bound to make the observation that Scottish women are different from Scottish men.

> The girls an the boys don't mix much. Girls like organisin. We used to have parties if someone was goin away in our class, an it was always the girls that organised it. Boys like fightin. If there's any fightin, it's always roun the back o the school; an ye jus see a big crowd stampedin, an they jus make a circle roun them, an if the two people fightin move away, the circle jus moves wi them.
>
> STEVEN RUSSELL, *11*, *Wallace High School, Stirling*

The rest of us might be struggling with our modern attitudes, but those nearer either end of the age spectrum are clear on the distinction.

> It's all women that work here. Any charity thing, it's usually women that do it. And it's mostly ladies' clothes we do. An to be quite honest, a lot o women don't like the idea of men sortin women's clothes. An I can quite understand that. It doesn't seem quite natural.
>
> ANNE MINTO, *55*, *shop assistant, Oxfam, Falkirk*

It's easy to forget what a recent thing it is, the revolution which has seen women's place in the world transformed. It's only since the 1870s that most girls have been going to secondary school, or able to go to university. Only since 1928 that women have had the vote on the same terms as men. And women ministers and elders only began to be permitted by the Kirk in the 1960s.

> I did mostly shop work for many years. That was your life in those days – it was out of school and into a shop, unless your parents could afford to put ye into college or university. And I

was brought up on a farm, and it was really a case of ye had to leave school to help pay for your other brothers and sisters.

SANDRA TULLOCH, *53, office cleaner, Inverness*

Things have changed, certainly; but maybe not as much as we'd imagine. In places which are stubborn in their resistance to change and diversity, the same traditions which have bonded many of us together make us dismally inflexible. Mix that with a history of tough-guy heroes and women kept 'in their place,' and there's little hope of Scotland leading the way in progressive attitudes to women (or, say, homosexuals).

> He is killin me by inches
> Treats me like a bloody slave
> When he dies o drink I'll miss him
> And I'll dance upon his grave.
>
> Street rhyme

It's a dangerous business, making generalisations about people. Our culture often does the job for us, and on this particular issue the traditions are clear: men are men, and women – mums, wives and girls.

At the start ma wife wasnae too keen on the boys boxin, because it's a bloodsport an it's hard an it's violent, ye know.

MICHAEL MURPHY, *47, district ranger, Forgewood Amateur Boxing Club, Motherwell*

If I had it my way I'd be trainin an playin football every night o the week. My wife says – hold on, ye've got tae spend some time wi me!

KEVIN PARR, *24, postman, Dundee*

My mum's been tae one fight, an she'll no be back tae another! She gets all keyed up, an because the other boy looks tough, she gets all worried, an it just adds tae the pressure.

GERARD MURPHY, *17, light welterweight, Forgewood Amateur Boxing Club, Motherwell*

Sport in Scotland is typical of the wider picture. Women are beginning to move onto playing fields where they were previously unimaginable, like football and rugby grounds. But their welcome has sometimes been frosty. Even the golf clubs which you might imagine would be relatively genteel havens for their 28,000 lady members, are often fortresses of chauvinism. In 1996 Drumpelier Golf Club in Coatbridge turned down £47,778 in lottery money towards a new clubhouse, rather than give equal rights to lady members (a requirement of lottery fund grants).

Now it's important to try and be fair-minded here. Resistance is a perfectly understandable reaction from people (men) who face having something (their own way) taken away from them. It's true that there are a few ladies-only golf clubs, too, in Aberdeen, Fife, and Troon, and other places. And it's true, also, that many women, like many men, respect formal distinctions and separations between the sexes, even if they have their disadvantages.

> The lady bowlers have a waterproof wraparound skirt an a top an what-have-ye. But ye're no allowed tae wear trousers, which means the water drips off the skirt and down the legs an into the shoes. An that can be a bit of a nuisance. But I think, Scottish ladies' bowls, if there's a uniform, ye stick to it.
>
> ANNA SHERIDAN, 67, *Fort Matilda Bowling Club, Greenock*

The problem arises with the much bigger game. There's no avoiding the impression that the ideas of tradition and personal choice which are used to justify cherished inequalities, are also the arguments used by men who want to hang onto much more fundamental privileges. At women's expense.

And in the bigger game, in shops and offices, in the home and on the factory floor, women are still starting yards behind the pace. 'Woman's work' is by no means an outdated cliche. It's a perfectly accurate way of describing the poorer-paid, less secure, drearier end of the jobs market which is mostly avoided by men – shopwork, secretarial jobs, institutional catering, and so on.

> I did my hairdressin training, an when I was twenty-one or twenty-two I set up my own business in part of my mum's house in Dunshelt. It used to be my father's workroom and we converted it. Styles By Alex. It was really to supplement a widow's pension an help us get along, an I did it for just over three years. A lot o hard work. But I wasn't a businessman. I was far too soft.
>
> ALEX ALLAN, 33, *hairdresser, Birnam*

There's all different types do the check-outs. I'm the oldest, maybe even in the whole shop. It's terrible, but I don't think a lot realise it and there's a few catching up on me. It's all girls, really. At the moment there's one schoolboy, but I think they just don't think it's a male thing to do.

KATHLEEN CAMPBELL, *50, supermarket check-out operator, Dingwall*

I was obviously just one o these types who was destined to be a hairdresser. I started as an apprentice in Stirling straight from school for £3 a week, sweepin floors and gettin teas and coffees, an I was in seventh heaven. And as I keep sayin to the girls, it's a job ye've got to love. Ye could go an stack shelves an get £80 or £90 in your hand, an no job satisfaction at all. But I love this.

ANNE CAMERON, *38, hairdresser, Pitlochry*

One of the big changes in the jobs market over the last thirty years has been the huge increase in part-time work. In 1971, there were 270,000 Scots in part-time employment; at the end of 1997 the number was 630,000, and four out of every five of that number was a woman. (Over the same period, the number of women in full-time jobs actually fell.)

After I had my family I went into catering part-time, and then I heard about a cleaning job from half-past-four to half-past-six, for a few extra pennies. Ye have your feather-duster and duster and polisher and vacuum cleaner, and a buffer for polishing the floors. And when I started, the buffer used to take off with me. It was dreadful; the operator used to have to come and switch it off for me. But it's all right now. It was just a case of using the loaf, as one would say. And it opens your eyes, this job. Ye just don't think that people can do some of the things they do. One of my pet hates is chewing-gum in a bin – it's one of the most revolting things. I don't think people realise that somebody has to come along and clean up after them. But ye build up a bit of a relationship with the girls and the boys in the office – they're not a bad bunch. I do tick them off, but they give me as good back. And a lot of these men in the offices, ye'd think they'd no homes to go to; ye clean round them and use the feather flicker. And I try to chase them out early on a Friday: 'What are your wives going to think . . . ?'

SANDRA TULLOCH

Up here there's hotel work, etcetera, but it's all women's jobs, women's wages. You need two or three jobs to keep yourself going, you know?

JO MACKAY, *50, postbus driver, Durness*

The situation today has parallels with the way women are brought out of the home and into the workplace during war-time. A large number of men have been finding their traditional skills no longer required, while many employers have been gearing to cheap part-time workers. And, as in the past, it's women who have taken up the wage-earning slack.

But it's difficult to use fashionable words like empowerment for what's happened to the new working woman. Ideas like the 'glass ceiling' (a term for the invisible discrimination which prevents women rising beyond a certain point in the corporate hierarchy) are just a detail in the wider scene. The jobs most women are likely to find are a world away from the boardroom, doing plain, hard work which pays them less well than most men.

I've cleaned in schools, supermarkets, shops, offices. Now, I get up at half past four, and come out at five to do the switch room at British Telecom, when there's only a few operators on. Then I'm back home about half past seven and have something to eat, and then I go off to another job at half past eight, cleaning a furniture warehouse until one o'clock. Then I come home, and I come back out to British Telecom at half past three – and this time I go upstairs to the canteen and do all that area, and finish at half past six. Ye've got to be organised, and by Friday night I need the weekend. I do most of my work in the house on a Saturday. And I always keep Sunday for myself – to go for a run, or out for a bar lunch or something.

CATHERINE ALLAN, *51, office cleaner, Inverness*

Hairdressing is a very physically demanding job. It's long hours, ye start early an finish late, and ye're on your feet all day. You get paid a forty-hour week, but ye work forty-six or forty-eight, and do without lunches.

ALEX ALLAN

Here's a stark fact: women in Scotland are much more likely to be poor than men. What happens with jobs is the most obvious reason. In 1996, the average Scottish woman's annual pay for full-time employment was a little over £13,600 before tax. The average man earned close to £19,000. The yawning discrepancy is there right down to the lowest-paid work.

But there are other factors, too. Women's life expectancy is about six years longer than men's,[1] so there are many more single female pensioners living on very little money. When they're younger, too, if parents separate, the woman is nine times more likely than the man to find herself looking after any children, and trying to meet the expenses.

For it's clear that motherhood remains high on the agenda for most women.

It's just women. Women just get broody, d'ye know what I mean? They don't think about it till they're in the labour ward. But as soon as ye've had the baby ye just forget all about the pain. Two seconds before, ye're screamin your head off, it's just one o those things, an about five minutes after ye've delivered it, it's just the best feelin in the world. This is definitely the last one, though. Mind you, I said that after the first. And the second.

HEATHER SMYTH, 24, *Cumbernauld*

I'd been married to Stephen five years, an we'd just enjoyed life, doin what we want an havin a couple o holidays every year. We were always the kind o couple that if we just felt like goin out for a meal or goin to the pictures, we just got up an went. But I'm well into bein termed an 'old' mother now, an it jus comes to the point when ye feel ye're ready to plan a family. We said – if we don't do it now, we'll never do it.

MAUREEN BRIDGES, 31, *personnel officer, Mount Vernon, Glasgow*

I wasnae wantin any more weans efter Jim an Ashley. But then I met Michael, an I realised I did want one tae him. Money is a bit o a worry, cause Michael smashed his leg fallin off scaffoldin three years ago, an he's still waitin on his industrial claim comin through. But as we say, we'll get by. We'll manage.

PAULINE MONTGOMERY, 25, *Glasgow Royal Maternity Hospital*

Is this breeding business biological, or social? Is it personal, or part of the network of relationships that carries us all through the generations? Certainly, there seems to be the technology for women now to conceive a child without involving anything as messy as a man. But on the whole, settling-down-and-having-kids is something women want to do in partnership. Is that bad?

Still, when the light shines a certain way it looks very much as if motherhood itself can end up turning into yet another wrinkle for keeping women in their place. There are few house-husbands. Decent childcare and nursery provision is the one facility which can free women from the obligation to be unequal, and Scotland's far behind in this department, too. Only the most enlightened businesses have anything like a company creche, and council measures are thoroughly poor. So, the pressure falls particularly on those who can't afford to pay for help with their children.

> I worked up to deputy manager of a shop in Stirling, an then I had the chance to lease the shop here in '88. Then I had a baby, who was in the salon with me for a year and a half, an it was gettin too much. In the likes of Perth an the top salons a lot o the hairdressers are men, an I suppose what happens is we get married and have children, an we never get to the top.
>
> ANNE CAMERON

> I'm lucky I've had the chances I've had so far. I started as a cleaner in 1987, and now I'm a business planner. I had a baby last year, though, and I feel as if I'm fightin against the tide sometimes. We don't go and visit people or go away at weekends as much as we used to. But I've got a really good child-minder now, so no worries.
>
> SHONA MACDONALD, 30, *business planner, Clunie power station, Pitlochry*

> I probly get five an a half or six hours' sleep a day, wi workin here an lookin after Michelle, who's three, an doin the shoppin an that, dependin on what shift ma husband's on. It's no as much as I'd like. But I make up for it at the weekends.
>
> MARIE CUNNINGHAM, 26, *machine operator, Peterhead*

Of course, the women who make the difficult decision to take a job as well as looking after their children will suffer other prejudices into the bargain. More than a few folk would say girls like that don't know their place: with their babies. And it's curious to see many of the feminists whose militancy beat the phrase sexual discrimination into the conscience of the wider world in the 1960s – like Germaine Greer, or Fay Weldon – taking a markedly softer line these days.

For there's a long, long way to go before the old prejudices fade away. It was bad enough to find politicians beginning to talk without embarrassment in the last years of the 1990s Tory government about things like 'better mothering' and 'freeing women from the workplace.' Even from the room with the blue wallpaper – and I'm not just saying this because I want to be freed from the workplace – it doesn't look like it's time yet for this tide to turn.

Unless you believe the dreams of mothers should stop at motherhood.

In the past ye'd maybe hear some people sayin – you've got no right to be workin when ye've got a child to look after. An we probly could manage financially if I didn't go back to work. But I just feel I would have to have more in ma life. When ye're not workin, every day runs into the next, an the weekends all run in together, an it's quite difficult to come to terms with that. Havin said that, everythin's just so new. Maybe I won't be able to bear leavin Lauren with ma sister when it comes down to it.

MAUREEN BRIDGES

I've been very lucky, I've been able to be a part-time mother, wife, dog-trainer and vet, so I suppose my epitaph could be 'part-time'. But it wouldn't really work with ma husband's job, if I was full-time. We'd hardly see each other.

PATRICIA WOOD, 45, *vet, Aberdeen*

I was workin in a clothin factory fae when I came out of school in '79, an then in '88 I had a baby. But I knew I'd be back out; for the money, an to better masel, an tae get all the nice things ye wanted.

SUSAN GRANT, 31, *machine operator, Levi Strauss, Bellshill*

Amidst all the juggling of responsibilities, the one saving grace about 'women's work' is that it breathes life into the community of women who might once have seen each other at the wash-house or the drying green. There's consolation and support in the network of friendships at work. And a break from the routine, in the girls' night out.

There's four of us here at a time, and we have a good laugh. We're all goin out to Mackay's Hotel on Saturday to celebrate my birthday, and have a couple o drinks and a game o pool.
LYNN JACKSON, *17, trainee, Hair Studio, Pitlochry*

It's quite snug in the basement, where we're gradin an pricin the donated goods that comes in. We have a laugh. It's – What do ye think about this? Imagine anybody gettin rid o this! Do ye remember when we wore these? We had an awful silly pair o trousers came in last week, with yellow flowers on, a wee bit kind o raucous an kind o baggy, an one o us went upstairs wearin them, to give the customers a laugh.
DIANE FERRIE, *shop assistant, Oxfam, Falkirk*

We all get on really well, it's a real community in the super-market. We're all married an have families, an I've been up to a couple o their houses for blethers an that. An I know some o the young girls, who have been in class wi ma boys. I think one o them used to go out wi one o them. But I dinnae bother.
JOYCE CAMERON, *43, checkout operator, Dingwall*

The harsh reality about whatever improvements there have been to the opportunities of Scottish women is that, like most changes which help the disadvantaged, they were brought about by confrontation. Women literally would not have won the vote if it hadn't been for the suffragettes, whose tactics in Scotland ranged from campaigning against Winston Churchill in his prospective 1908 parliamentary seat of Dundee, to burning Leuchars railway station and several other landmarks. In 1913, two suffragettes hid on the golf course at Lossiemouth and assaulted Asquith, the Prime Minister of the time.

Confrontation's a fair word to describe the time in 1996 when two local girls on horseback gatecrashed the men-only Hawick Common Riding. No doubt the intrusion to this ritual celebration will have saddened quite a few well-meaning folk, and unbalanced a smaller number whose vicious vitriol is hard to forgive. But the bravery of Mandy Graham and Ashley Simpson in the face of a lengthy community and media stramash brought about the beginnings of a change which many other people wanted. (And not even that big a change; women had been involved in the Common Ridings before 1932, when they were banned.)

It's not easy though, being at the sharp end of confrontation. It means calling on personal resources which may mean very little to those who follow happily once the barriers have been pulled back. Many women in Scotland are pioneers, and know something of what's involved. And, tough as it is, there'll have to be pioneers for some time to come.

It used tae be just the men bowlers went tae play the like of the Grangemouth clubs, but when they started tae get short o people, maself an another lady went with them. We played an all-male green, an we had tae get special dispensation tae play; it caused a lot o commotion at the time.

JEAN WHITEFORD, 63, *retired clerical worker, Fort Matilda Bowling Club, Greenock*

I never ever thought I'd be a train driver. But I worked in the Strathclyde Transport canteen for two years, an then moved into the underground ticket offices, an then drivin was the next step. Sometimes if ye're out socially, people say – ye're a train driver? No, it can't be right. But it doesn't seem very unusual to me. Though sometimes if somebody gets stuck in the doors or there's a signal fault or somethin, ye see them: 'Bloody typical woman driver.' Aaargh! Don't say that to me! I do like the job, but it's seven years now, an I'm gettin a bit fed up with it. Hopefully, I'll be able to move on to being a stationmaster, in charge of a station.

LESLEY QUIGLEY, 29, *underground train driver, Glasgow*

When I went on courses an things ye did get the ones who think the worst thing on earth ye could be was female, civilian, an workin for the police – the old dyed-in-the-wool police officers that didn't think women had much of a role to play. But everybody's been very friendly here.

KATHLEEN HENDERSON, 34, *scenes of crime officer, Dumfries and Galloway Police*

Ye really get led on at the careers office, there's so much crap involved it's mad, and once you actually join a ship it's a bit of a shock – down on your hands an knees scrubbin floors, an ye barely get any sleep, it's just a nightmare. There were twenty-one Wrens on HMS *Sirius* out of 240, an we were gettin a lot o stick from the boys at first. The girls have to work harder just to prove themselves, an it's hard, fire-fightin with big bottles on your back, or throwin heavin lines an big wire ropes, or loadin big boxes, ye just get covered in bruises. But once we'd been to sea an the watch was workin together, it was fine. We had a really good ship's company, an they look after ye. An it's grand, especially when ye get into a foreign port. I've been to the States, Canada, Denmark, Tunisia, Portugal. Ma family think it's great, gettin postcards from all over the place on the mantelpiece in Aberdeen. I didn't join up to make a career of it, though. In ten years' time I'll hopefully be married with kids – if somebody'll have me.

ABLE WREN DEBBIE WISHART, 22, *Royal Navy, Rosyth*

Well, it'd be wrong to suggest that women are the only ones to find things difficult these days. All of the ongoing changes and renegotiations make life more of a challenge for men, to be sure. As we like to complain, at the very least, women are – different, these days, somehow.

It is difficult to switch off from the job. I'm not the most interesting person to go out with on a Saturday night – 'Did you see the state of those wash-hand basins in the toilets?' My husband's a poor suffering soul, so he is.

MARIA CORRIGAN, 26, *food control officer, East Kilbride*

There's the story of the Aberdeen woman watching a young man pushing a pram around Duthie Park. He's murmuring reassuringly to the pram's occupant as he goes: 'That's it, Darren, ye're deein fine. Jist relax. Ye're deein gran. Nae bother, Darren. It'll be OK.' The woman's impressed. 'You fairly now how to speak to a baby,' she says. 'And what seems to be the matter with wee Darren, anyway?' 'No,' says the young dad. 'He's Alan. I'm Darren.'[2]

And it's true that there's been a fair bit of pioneering on the other side of the sex war, as well.

It's been difficult, bein a male nurse, tae say the least. Initially it's a shock to the system, an a lot o people say – I don't know how ye manage it. But ye get used tae it, an there's more males comin into nursin now. Maybe some female patients are embarrassed tae have a male nurse, too, an it's their right tae say if they don't want one. But a lot o them love it; ye can see their eyes lightin up when ye come intae the wards.

STAFF NURSE JOHN ROBB, 28, *Crosshouse Hospital, Kilmarnock*

NOTES

1. In the late 1990s, the average Scot can expect to live to around 72 (men) or 78 (women).
2. From a story told by Ethel Baird of Kincorth, collected by Robbie Shepherd and Norman Harper in *A Dash O' Doric*, Canongate Books, 1995.

Anyone That's Got Children
Will Know
SOCIAL STRAINS

Overwhelmingly, the one word common to almost every voice in this book is 'change.' It's the way of things that a small amount of change affects our perspective much more dramatically than a large amount of stability. But there's a recurring, troubling note in many people's stories, when they're talking about what life's like; an almost universal sense that the old ways, the familiar, and the secure, are slipping from our grasp.

And by any standards it's possible to measure, it does really look as if the pace of change in our institutions, business, science and technology, social standards and environment has never been more dizzying.

I don't think there's such a thing nowadays as total job security. Ye just have to hope that what ye're doin is useful. We've got a review comin up, and it does affect ye, ye think, what's goin to be the future? But ye just have to do the best ye can.

SHONA MACDONALD, 30, *business planner, Clunie power station, Pitlochry*

I was an engineer all ma life. I worked at a wee foundry in Dalkeith, an then latterly I was at Ferranti's for thirteen years. Ye were workin tae Ministry targets, full tilt all the time, an in millionths; it's a wee bit stress-related, ye're havin tae concentrate all the time. Then I got made redundant. An it isnae half different here. Ye havnae got the pressure, your ain discipline's entirely different. An it's a nice clean job for a change, ye're no comin' home stinkin o machine oil an that, the wife's no got dirty clothes tae wash. Ye get tae know everybody, an it's a type o group an that, ye soon learn that ye fit in. It's about three years I've been away from the tools now, an I'd find it awfy hard tae go back tae them.

JOHN ARNOTT, 53, *warder, Gallery of Modern Art, Edinburgh*

I'm fae Embra, an came up here for ma mum an dad's work. Ma dad works in the prison, an ma mum works in a hoose where handicapped folk bide, like. Well, Peterheid's alright, but I wouldnae like to be here for the rest o ma life. Aebody kens each other's business, like. I dinna think it's an awfy friendly place.

JENNY McCONNELL, *18, machine operator, Peterhead*

Ye're always lookin over your shoulder. But a few years ago I realised that it's no good in worryin, or ye'd probably be in a coffin by now. Ye worried an worried. Put it this way, I was gettin paid off, ye're no in control of your destiny, an . . . Ye've got tae be philosophical about it.

JAMIE WEBSTER, *43, welder, Govan*

Where the change is actually coming from is a different matter. Decisions will be taken in some office or committee room a long, long way from here; company headquarters in Tokyo or New York, maybe; US strategic command in the Pentagon; the Bundesbank; a departmental conference in Brussels. Layer on layer of international economic and political trade-offs smother any clear picture of why things are different when we wake up in the morning, as if – like the technology we all depend on – the human world has become too complex for any one person to understand.

When I got my redundancy payment from Ravenscraig, I bought nothin, we had no fancy holidays . . . because I thought: right, we'll just live on this until I have a proper job. An I put five thousand pounds into an account in London, an that was to be for my youngest daughter's weddin, my darlin Siobhan. But only after a while ye thought, hang on, how long is this goin to last? It seems like a lot o money, but it's only two years' wages. An I went to every single agency, job clubs, job matchin, or whatever, an I applied for virtually anythin – I actually applied for a job as a caretaker in a tower block. An I did not even get a response from anyone, for a full year. There was a stigma, a feelin that because ye're ex-Ravenscraig, an ye've got a whack o money in the bank, ye're goin to be a liability. An that was the depression of it, watching the redundancy money comin down an down an down, an bein helpless. An then, havin to dip into that five

thousand pounds. An then, every penny's gone. An ye have
to go cap-in-hand, an ask for support.

DOUGLAS SILVESTER, 47, *part-time lecturer, Wishaw*

The feeling of dislocation from a properly ordered environment is
familiar in modern times. And when the security of community
and tradition are under attack, our lack of leadership in matters
of ethics and values reveals an uncomfortable space. The decline
of an authoritative church and our educational system has left us
failing to answer questions about the world and what it's for which
the old Kirk dominie would have tripped off without a thought, and
likely a skelp to the questioner's ear for good measure.

It's not that the dominie's answer was necessarily right; but a
woolly half-answer just doesn't do the trick.

When I was on rummage crews in Dundee in '68 we'd never
found drugs before – and we started to find drugs. And it's
really mushroomed since then. It blossomed in '72 to '82, and
now, it's frightenin. Anyone that's got children will know . . .
I feel quite sorry, we sometimes go into the inner-city deprived
areas where people are usin drugs to relieve the pain of not
havin work or money, and it's quite hard. We do see people
who are ill through drugs, so we understand the pain and
suffering they cause.

JOHN FOTHERINGHAM, 47, *Customs and Excise officer,*
Grangemouth

Whatever our painful social problems, it's no longer apt to picture
Scotland as an alcoholic. (Our per capita alcohol consumption in the
1990s is actually a little less than that in England.) The Caledonian
brain is as likely to be addled with heroin (injected or smoked), cocaine,
cannabis, ecstasy, LSD, uppers, downers or any of the myriad of
laboratory-produced chemicals. Drug-taking in Scotland is proportionately more prevalent than in the rest of Britain, and the rates for
individual drugs are among the highest in Europe.

We do get a lot of patients from drink and drugs problems,
and you sometimes think what else can we do, that these
problems are not so rampant? It's a social problem, and it's
actually growing more and more.

SISTER FARLEY WEIR, 40, *Crosshouse Hospital,*
Kilmarnock

The statistics of the change to alternative drugs are the sort of thing any booming business would kill for: there were 249 notified drug addicts in Scotland in 1981. In 1994, there were 3691. Over the same period of time, the number of seizures of controlled drugs by police and Customs officers increased tenfold. The reason for Edinburgh becoming the 'AIDS capital of Europe' in the 1980s was nothing to do with homosexuals. It stemmed from needle-sharing among heroin users in the city's outlying council estates.

But drugs have become part of our culture, and it's entirely open to question whether the illegal drugs do as much harm as the highly marketed, wealth-generating traditional ones. And in the absence of a credible stance on the subject from the law-makers, a hypocritical cloud of criminality hangs over a very big part of our population. Which is a shame, because there's plenty of clouds of criminality as it is.

There was a taxi-driver got murdered by a passenger five years ago, an it always sticks in our minds. That really brought it home to every taxi driver in the town – that our job is a job where we're at risk wi the public. If ye get a guy that looks a bit rough an gets in the back an sits directly behind ye, the hair on the back o your neck starts to stand on end. Your mind's racin at times.

BRIAN McINTOSH, *38, taxi driver, Aberdeen*

Ye always tend to look for the best in people, but in this job ye realise that there are some pretty nasty ones around. I think any time ye go to somethin like a murder scene, ye do see aspects of people that ye wouldn't normally. An I think I have become a bit cynical; ye're more likely to meet someone an think – well, what's your angle? It's like – expect the worst in people, an ye won't be disappointed.

KATHLEEN HENDERSON, *34, scenes of crime officer, Dumfries and Galloway Police*

Your eye becomes your judge, an ye can usually spot the bad ones. Women, couples – no trouble. But more than one guy, I want to know where they're sittin, so I can keep an eye on them. Though even if somebody wants to be a bit aggressive, ye can usually talk them out of it.

BRIAN O'NEILL, *49, taxi driver, Aberdeen*

It's really not credible to claim that crime is nothing to do with poverty, homelessness, unemployment, and alienation. Over the same period that the number of recorded violent crimes in Scotland increased by forty percent, the number of applications to local authorities for homes virtually trebled (43,000 in 1994) and so did local authority spending on social work. Again, these were the years in the '80s and '90s when the poorest people in Scotland were growing poorer (while the richest, incidentally, grew richer).

The issue drags at the well-being of the whole country, and yet the problems can be identified with eerie precision in the poorest parts of our cities. In the housing scheme of Craigmillar (one of the places whose 'shooting galleries' bred the 1980s Edinburgh AIDS epidemic), one girl in four will have a child before she is twenty. A few miles away in well-heeled Murrayfield, the figure is nearer one in two hundred. Statistically, the Craigmillar girl can expect to die several years before her Murrayfield counterpart. Glasgow has souped up its image with marketing puffs like the Garden Festival (1988), City of Culture (1990) and the City of Architecture (1999), but it remains a place where sixty percent of the children are so disadvantaged that they get clothing grants.

The inequalities, moral fudges, crime and urban depersonalisation have all been factors in the escape to rural Scotland, particularly among parents.

We were in Portobello, an we'd been out lookin for Caroline Hogg when she went missin. It brings it home tae ye. Ye've got tae give them as secure a first half of their life as ye can.
STEWART SOMERVILLE, *30, swimming pool supervisor,*
Hoy[1]

Maybe it is better to be at a distance from some o the things that go on in the cities. But it's always creepin closer. Even Hawick has its drugs problems these days.
LINDA DOUGLAS, *28, farmer's wife, Ruletownhead*

Persistent social ills present the biggest challenge to the vision which could carry Scotland into the future. But the answer to the problems is staring us in the face with their local nature; all of us know that the security which the refugees are finding in the country, and which has been lost in parts of our cities, lies in community.

NOTES

1. Caroline Hogg was one of several young girls who were abducted and murdered by a Scottish lorry driver in one of the most disturbing series of crimes in the 1980s.

Nobody to Say No
VALUES AND OPPORTUNITIES

Perhaps it comes from a history of hard times, but Scottish traditions have always tended towards the belief that people in need should be looked after. Scots contribute proportionately more to charity than many wealthier nations, and we are one of the few populations in the world which still voluntarily donates enough blood to treat its sick.

Compared to England, twice as many young people proportionately graduate in health-related fields, and these skills have attracted a vigorous core of clinical research, bio-science and healthcare companies. Long after Simpson and Fleming's pioneering work with anaesthetics and antibiotics, Scots are still making breakthroughs in healing; Ian Donald pioneered obstetric ultrasound, while Sir James Black won the Nobel prize for his invention of the life-saving beta-blocker. And in the 1990s, Scottish scientists have been among the worldwide elite who are pushing back a vast new frontier in the search for the most fundamental roots of human diseases and defects in our inherited genetic codes.

When I started studying genetics it was a quiet little backwater. At that time it was not so much human genetics, but animal breeding and mouse genetics. And in the last ten years it's grown enormously, become hectic and competitive and important. In about 1984 we were the first to map a gene which causes retinitis pigmentosa, a form of tunnel vision – and to cut a long story short, we're still working on it. The mapping is like saying it's in this chapter of this book, whereas identifying the specific gene is like finding one letter in the chapter. It's taken far longer than we thought, but we're very close now – as are other groups overseas. It's a very, very competitive field now, but it would be wonderful to be the first. Funding is a big problem. I started off here with just myself, and a lot of the time has been spent struggling to get more skilled help and more funds, and building up resources to the point where we're in a position to compete with much bigger resources elsewhere.

DR ALAN WRIGHT, 46, *research team leader, Human Genetics Unit, Western General Hospital, Edinburgh*

On the front-line of this people-oriented business, the post-war National Health Service has become a part of everybody's life in a way which would have been unimaginable fifty years ago. As recently as the 1960s it was so common for Scottish mothers to give birth at home that the patient population of places like Glasgow Royal Maternity Hospital – known as The Rottenrow, after its address at numbers 147-163 in that street – was predominantly high-risk cases. Now, some 5000 Scots come into the world every year at The Rottenrow, and ninety-nine percent of mothers leave with their babies 'both well'.

I've got five sisters an three brothers, an four o them was born in the hoose. But when I fell pregnant wi Jim, I asked ma sisters that had had weans – an this place was recommended.

PAULINE MONTGOMERY, 25, *Glasgow Royal Maternity Hospital*

The health service has been under strain for some time, though, and as the post-war 'baby boom' – the late middle-aged generation who outnumber any other – begin to move into the age bracket where they will need plenty of attention, the pressure will grow. The trend has been towards cutting the number of patients in hospital, and the number of hospital beds in Scotland fell from around 60,000 in 1984 to around 41,000 twelve years later, with advances in treatment and increased care in the community credited for the reduction. Yet during this same period, the numbers of both GPs, and home visits by district nurses, barely rose. And there are still waiting-lists of many thousands, and beds in hospital corridors.

Like teachers, the caring professions have had to cope with a succession of changes in the philosophy, techniques and management of their jobs, in addition to the endless research-driven changes in medicine. The job of looking after people in need these days comes with other, less fulfilling challenges.

Nursin has got a more professional profile than in days gone by. It's not as old-fashioned as when Matron was about, an ye didn't say a word, an your shoes were always pointin in the right direction, an ye didn't look at a doctor in a certain way. But the climate's really changin now, an nobody knows what's round the corner. The tradition is it was a job for life; but we have to change our thoughts that way.

RHONA SCOTT, *25, coronary care nurse, Crosshouse Hospital, Kilmarnock*

I'm in my last year of an honours course in management with the Open University, but it's very difficult to think where I want to go. The Trust here have created all these new management posts, and you don't have to be a nurse – these people are coming from all sorts of other professions. But I don't want to leave the health service. It's my home.

SISTER FARLEY WEIR, *40, Crosshouse Hospital, Kilmarnock*

Ma father was a nurse. An I seen what ma dad was involved in wi the Health Service, an I wanted tae keep away from it! No, that's a bit of a joke. I've been in nursin really all ma life. An ye can see the pressures o the job, an the politics of it. There have certainly been major changes in the last few years. Sometimes ye do feel ye're bein taken away from the bedside, with low staffin levels an sickness an things, paperwork and accountability ... Sometimes there's not enough hours in the day tae do what ye want tae do, an I don't see that improvin, tae be honest. An the change process is very stressful, with the Trust, an new models of nursin, an constantly learnin an readin an keepin up tae date. I've got a couple o young kids now, an when they're at school an I'm workin most weekends, it's hard.

STAFF NURSE JOHN ROBB, *28, Crosshouse Hospital, Kilmarnock*

The difficulties in the field of patient care are an unhappy state of affairs in a nation which still has a reputation for excellence in medical matters. For the truth of it is that despite the decline of the church and moral leadership, and many years of government based on the Thatcherite philosophy of self-advancement, communal values remain important. Perhaps it's not surprising that Margaret Thatcher's 'there is no such thing as society' never caught on in a place where ideas of belonging have been ingrained through long hardships.

I love it, working here. Whenever any of the famines or disasters happen, you think – well, I'm doing a wee bit to help. It makes you sleep easier in your bed at night, because it could just as easily be you as them.

DIANE FERRIE, *shop assistant, Oxfam, Falkirk*

I would like to work full-time for a charity, now. To be a mother and not be able to provide for your children because of famine or war or sheer poverty must be so heart-rending; I can't imagine what it would be like. But the Government is cutting back on a lot of projects, and unfortunately it has to be the do-gooders that take these things on.

LINDA CONWAY, *trading convener, Oxfam, Falkirk*

Of course it's simple-minded to attempt any sort of pseudo-scientific quantification of the spirit of community. But in a mood of simple-minded enthusiasm, let me offer a small anecdote.

Researchers recently surveyed 34,000 senior and middle managers from businesses around the world in an attempt to define the cultural attitudes which underly regional economic fortunes.[1] The academics were surprised to discover that the 250 Scots surveyed had more in common with the team-based values of the Eastern nations than the competitive ethics of the West. In answer to the ponderous question 'Is quality of life improved by gaining as much freedom as possible and the maximum opportunity to develop oneself or by continuously taking care of one's fellow man even when it obstructs individual freedom and development?' some fifty-seven percent of the Scots opted for their fellow man. The relative figure for English respondents was thirty-eight percent; the Americans rated thirty percent.

I've always wanted tae focus on workin wi the elderly. It's no an attractive area for nursin; a lot o the young girls want tae look for the acute episodes an the monitors an all that, like accident an emergency ye see on the television. But if ye look at the demographics, the population is goin tae continue tae rise, so it's a big area. An it's really fascinatin tae hear what the elderly patients have tae say. They've been through a lot, they're characters in themselves. They've been through two world wars, some o them, an they've given a lot to society. An they deserve a lot back.

JOHN ROBB

What gets me out in the mornins is doin a school run. Central Taxis doesn't rely on the oil companies like a lot o them – most of our work is hospital patients and contract work for handicapped children an the sick children's hospital. Morning an afternoon five days a week I take two six year-olds and one ten year-old to school. They have learnin difficulties, an one girl has Down's Syndrome. An it gets to the stage where one of the boys comes up an gives me a hug an that sort of thing, an it's as much a pleasure as it is a job.

BRIAN McINTOSH, *38, taxi driver, Aberdeen*

Sometimes our pursuit of looking after our fellow man goes against commercial trends, and what everybody else is doing, and even what a lot of people would call logic.

In this area it's most often a body we have to take down. When people fall, they fall a great distance, an it's often head injuries. It is distressing. We usually meet an have a sort o debriefing a few days later, an it's good to get it out. But one incident that comes to mind, many years ago: a young child just wandered off on the hill, on a summer's evenin, only two years old, I think. An we did see some tiny footprints. It became dark, an the child had virtually no clothin – just a pair o shorts an a pair o welly boots. Eventually in the early hours o the mornin we did find him. An it was a tremendous feelin that he was fine. Tremendous.

JIM BUCHANAN, *41, mountain rescue team equipment officer, Dundonnell*

Every year, armies of climbers and walkers head for Scotland's hills – maybe a hundred thousand people on Easter weekend alone – and every year the list of fatalities is longer. Of course, the locals know that some mountains are killers; An Teallach, near Dundonnell in Wester Ross, takes a life about once a year. But when something goes wrong, the phone will ring in a local house, and a team of volunteers much like the Dundonnell collection of teachers, British Telecom engineers, oil workers, and local tradesmen, could be somebody's best chance of surviving.

And the unpaid rescuers all have stories of good days and bad days, out on their landscape, chasing strangers.

There's a particular path between Achiltibuie and north of Ullapool, a coastal path – very steep, very arduous, very difficult. On the map it doesn't look very much. But in the summer ye get people settin off at maybe half past three in the afternoon in shorts, no map, no food, no compass, no torch ... Ye can try to tell people, to warn them of the dangers, but there comes a point where some people just don't like advice.

NEVIS HULME, *36, mountain rescue team leader and teacher, Gairloch*

When ye're on a shout ye're kind o hyper, the adrenalin runs, and it's exciting. Afterwards, it hits you, especially if ye've been involved in bringin down a body. It's a bit of a shock, but ye get used to it. My first call-out was someone who had unfortunately died on the hills. She'd been dead for a number o months. An I'll always remember that.

DONALD MACRAE, *22, Dundonnell mountain rescue team, Gairloch*

I have dealt with many injuries, an fatalities. At the time ye may have to deal with distressed relatives, and rather ugly bodies, an it is just a job to be done. A couple o days later it dawns on you what's happened, an that can be upsetting for a while. But it's strange; ye often find the incidents where we save people's lives it's simply a thank-you letter, an that's it. The greatest appreciation comes from those when there's been a fatality an ye've brought a body down from the mountain. Or animal rescues. We recently had a dog that was trapped in a corrie for a week before we could get to it. And the delight we received that day ... The owner was just so grateful.

NEVIS HULME

Of course, it's nice to be nice. And most Scots, talking about a sense of common interest with their fellow men and women, would say that this is the correct way to be. But the point that the business analysts are making is that team-based values are a sounder foundation for long-term prosperity than individual ambitions. It seems as if what we have, our sense of common interest, is actually a very good starting-point for making things work successfully.

It's normally word o mouth that gets people workin here. If ye know of anybody that's retiring, ye say – oh, why don't you come an help us in the shop?

DIANE FERRIE

In the late 1990s, the first change of government at Westminster in eighteen years brings genuinely new prospects. Here's the party – though masterfully retailored for electoral advantage – whose socialist roots were in Scotland. What will the son of the manse (Gordon Brown) and the two Edinburgh schoolboys (Robin Cook and Tony Blair) brew up on the banks of the Thames?

Was that really the phrase – 'work-ethic', there?

Well, the single thing which can both express and protect our community values is local power. Only through taking control of the responsibilities on our doorstep can we resist marginalisation by the empires which, with the best will in the world, tend to exploit us. A Scottish parliament will do some of it; but there's no point in just moving the nanny state to Edinburgh. Power has to carry on going out to the edges.

This doesn't just mean more rural communities like Assynt and Eigg taking control of their resources. It's to do with parents and pupils and local people taking more responsibility for running schools; residents' groups having power over planning and transport policies in their area; employees having more involvement in the companies they work for, including profit-sharing and decision-making; communities having more control of the facilities they share, from allotments to housing schemes to leisure centres. It's to do with overcoming inertia to the point where the planners and the politicians never get a free rein again.

They look like shanty towns, a lot o the sites, just hung-up old hats an things. On our site, about a third are unemployed, about a third are pensioners, an they're up there every day in life. A lot o them have gas canister stoves tae make a cup o soup, an some o them have comfy chairs an things like that. It keeps them alive, it gives them somewhere tae go, and an interest. There's always somebody there tae talk to. It's just an uphill battle wi the council a' the time, they think it's just silly old men trundlin up an doon the garden path. They don't want tae take responsibility for the upkeep o the allotments. They just want them tae fade away. But in latter years, more an more women have been comin in. Quite a lot o the sites in Glasgow are run by women now. An here, we hold Christmas raffles, an buy people fertilisers an things like that, cause these things are so expensive. An last year we had an Easter dance, an it was wonderful, because all the old-timers wanted to come; the old spirit seemed to come back.

REBECCA BROWN, 45, *legal office assistant, Budhill and Springboig allotments, Glasgow*

There was really nothing here for us in the early days, except after the day shift coming home, up to the park and play football, and the usual patter sort of thing. And we said – 'We should get something here.' We decided that if we got 120 or 130 men to contribute threepence a week, and if we could guarantee that, somebody might come in with a grant. And the club was built, and a bowling green put in, and it turned into quite a nice club. And these days we call it a 'play school', all the redundant miners. We do carpet bowls on a Tuesday, dominoes, badminton if you can manage it, and at the end of the year we have a wee concert for ourselves, and we go a trip – Dunfermline, Berwick, different places. And now we have got this thing going up at the pit bing. They're putting a monument there, and it's coming up lovely with trees and what-have-you. It's pretty high up, and you can see right out to the Bass Rock and the bridge, Rosewell, Newtongrange, Carberry – it's a wonderful view. So we've got together, we've got an old hutch, and we're doing it up with a steel plate on top designated with the different areas, in memory of the Midlothian miners. It's quite a lovely walk up there now.

MAURICE TURNER, 74, *retired miner, Danderhall*

It's true, local democracy means committees, and meetings, and administration, and negotiation, and a lot of other habits for which we seem to have plenty of bad examples. Just look at Scotland's district councils. (There's the story of the west-coast councillor roused from the corner of the council chamber known as the 'boax-bed' by a proposal to do something for posterity. Raising himself to his full height, this fellow waits until he has the attention of the council: 'Ma Lord Proavist. It's high time fur tae ask wursels: whit has posterity ever done fur uz?')

But like democracy itself, a life of negotiation is the least worst of the options. Scotland today boasts more good models of community initiative and local power than at any time since industrialisation, and the trend is gaining momentum. In crofting townships, urban housing associations, village shops and a bagful of other settings, local co-operatives are coming together to take control for all sorts of good reasons.

> SPIRIT OF DEFIANCE LIGHTS THE STREETS
> In dignified silence, the mothers of Cranhill last night marched through the streets with candles to shed light on the lives of young people darkened by the evil of drug-dealing.
> It took the death of thirteen-year-old Alan Harper, Scotland's youngest heroin victim, to spur the women of the Glasgow estate to say enough was enough.
> Local councillor Gaille McCann spoke for them all as she declared: 'This is our community and we are taking it back.'
>
> *The Herald*, February 6, 1998

It's an important time for Scotland, a time of new beginnings, and new hopes for the future. And if you listen, you might hear a new confidence stirring. Amongst all the changes, as we grope our way towards something better, the simple fact is that every responsibility shouldered, every centralised dependency resisted, every sign of self-assertion and every challenge taken on is a firmer step towards maturity; a step which brings us further in from the edge.

> There's no rule book for this. We're workin on a voluntary basis, and I'm sure we've made mistakes, but we'll learn from those. We have had times where people have acted in a way which others haven't agreed with; some people will say we're too ambitious, and some people will say, what's in it for us? It's very difficult to spread the load, to spread the information and still do it effectively. And at the end of the day, ye only get a certain number of people to be directors. But we're still learning. And there is still a sense of feelin that we have control now; the landlord was always the one to say no. And there's nobody to say no, now.
>
> AILEEN KINNAIRD, 47, *teacher, Lochinver*

NOTES
1. *Mastering The Infinite Game*, Charles Hampden-Turner and Fons Trompenaars, Capstone, 1997.